YOUNGER THAN NEIL

ANHINGA PRESS

OTHER BOOKS BY EARL S. BRAGGS

In Which Language Do I Keep Silent
Anhinga Press, 2006

Crossing Tecumseh Street
Anhinga Press, 2003

House on Fontanka
Anhinga Press, 2000

Walking Back from Woodstock
Anhinga Press, 1997

Hat Dancer Blue
Anhinga Press, 1993

Hats
Linprint Press, 1989

YOUNGER THAN NEIL

POEMS

EARL S. BRAGGS

For Robert
for the voice
(your voice) I
heard today,
to you, these
poems, I
give.
Thanks
Earls
2-7-12
Chatta., TN

ANHINGA PRESS

Cover art: *Plantation Blues – Hopson Plantation, Clarksdale, MS*
photograph by Ron Anton Rocz
Author photograph: Natalie Strelnikova
Design, production, and cover design: C.L. Knight
Typesetting: Jill Runyan
Type Styles: titles set in Trajan Pro and text in Palatino

Library of Congress Cataloging-in-Publication Data
Younger Than Neil by Earl S. Braggs – First Edition
ISBN – 978-1-934695-12-8
Library of Congress Cataloging Card Number – 2009935035

This publication is sponsored in part by a grant
from the Florida Department of State,
Division of Cultural Affairs, and the Florida Arts Council.

Anhinga Press Inc. is a nonprofit corporation dedicated wholly to the
publication and appreciation of fine poetry and other literary genres.

For personal orders, catalogs
and information write to:
Anhinga Press
P.O. Box 10595
Tallahassee, Florida 32302
Web site: www.anhinga.org
E-mail: info@anhinga.org

Published in the United States
by Anhinga Press
Tallahassee, Florida
First Edition, 2009

For
Neil Young

The publication of this book is supported by a generous donation from Lavinia L. Johnson.

CONTENTS

Acknowledgments ix

ONE
Man Ray Photograph Surreal

A Long Glimpse Into the Surreal 3

TWO
Dry Weather Wars Zoo Storied Into a Desert Sand Box

The Night before Christmas: 21
Late for School 32

THREE
Carolina Storms Disguised by the Backdrop of Two East Coast Hurricanes

Storm Named Earl 45
Of Course, the Brochure Doesn't Mention Mrs. Abbot 49

FOUR
Black Boys in a Supermarket in California

A Supermarket in California 57

FIVE
Versions of the Shirt I Now Wear

Younger Than Neil 85

SIX
Freeway Exits and a One Tree Parking Lot
Essay

No Easy Silence 107

SEVEN
High-Yellow Night Nigger Roads

Monkey Junction, 1969 123
Mrs. Davis 127
The Cherokee in Me 130

EIGHT
Street Corner Boys and Two
Intersections on a Dead End One-way

The Wilmington Ten 135

NINE
Times Eleven Equals Twenty-Three

Before and After the AfterMATH: 9x11=23 147

About the Author 154

ACKNOWLEDGMENTS

Grateful acknowledgment to the editors of the following publications in which these poems first appeared, sometimes in different forms:

Cut Throat Magazine: "The Cherokee in Me"

Solo Cafe: Mrs. Davis

Tampa Review: "Before and After the AfterMATH (9x11=23)"

The poem, "A Storm Named Earl," appeared in the Cave Canem anthology, *The Ringing Ear (Black Poets Lean South)*, University of Georgia Press, 2007.

YOUNGER THAN NEIL

ONE

MAN
RAY
PHOTOGRAPH
SURREAL

A LONG GLIMPSE INTO THE SURREAL

(A Portrait of Lee Miller by Man Ray, 1930)

Let me ask you this.
Do you believe in silent naked black light?
Do you believe in the sad no color in the color
white?
Do you sometimes stop and stare
into the blank slate eyes of a photograph
and remember that you remember yourself
from somewhere, someplace
you've never been?

Have you ever been lost in streets, unfamiliar,
rumpled in a raincoat on a night of no rain?
Have you ever forgotten your last name?

Disband the Army

Now suppose I showed to you a portrait
of Lee Miller without
showing her portrait to you. Would you question
the dialogue between love and life long enough to believe
in me

and Man Ray walking half drunk because
Man Ray does not drink because Man Ray is dead as a blue pan.
Do you believe

in the unsilent color of the color red
blended out of context then blended slowly
into the slow motion movement of
slow cream three shades whiter than white
poured into the white

smoothness of her face? Lee Miller, her dress
black velvet crazy

juxtaposed, too lazy for a photographic pose
against the angle of her arm
just as white as white as ...
I am not. What we have here is

the elements of Dada surprise in the eyes of
a woman named Lee Miller. Do you believe in street signs?
I don't.
I believe in the orange color of oranges, not apples.
I believe I am lost like train station luggage,
a logarithmic suitcase
placed as an object, a still life

more still than "Please be still." A photograph
taken without a lens. Man Ray, 1930, New York City,
a room without a window. A picture of a woman, beauty

backdropped in mystery. Space
against nothing ordinary. A chair with no place to sit. Object

placed against object
manipulating
the optics of the camera, a transparent process of seeing
in between

Disband the Army

what is perceived and what is imagined. Man Ray
1930, New York City,
a room without a door.

A room in between the bridge
and the bridge.
A room facing the blue bottom
of a used up life. Someone planted a dull knife

in the third pocket of a rumpled raincoat
on a night of no rain. Sketches of Spain.

We, Man Ray, Lee Miller, and me
stumble together to keep from falling apart
together

Disband the Army

into the transformation of this blue night and that black night
blended into optics and lights and optics

that see clearly what lies beneath the feathers
of flying birds, words, my words confuse me
as much as they confuse themselves, and you

trust me because you do not trust me. Yet, we, you and I,
hold tight
against the wind blowing part way through
our working-class hairstyle, lifestyle.

We are the tactile, rebelling against the conventions of
convention.
We are the tactile, the transparent process of transparent
photographic printmaking
making us up with lipstick and a nightstick,

making us up to be unfamiliar
in the image of a familiar image
we cannot see.
Do you believe in beauty, a definition so soundly shared,
we can only disagree

Disband the Army

about the way a lover sees

a woman's eyes
a woman's lips
a woman's legs

long as displaced eroticism on a night of no rain?
Sketches of Spain.
Surrealism.

Dadaism
is the androgynous appearance of Marcel Duchamp,
content without context
context without surface.

Yet
Lee Miller stands upon nothing upon which to stand upon.
Let her return
like a street girl
flamboyant blonde, flamboyant brunette,
woman of thirty years,
the fugitive blue character of escaped love
escaping into the thin stale air of this night of no rain.
Sketches of Spain.
Logical conclusion is love's only enemy.

Disband the Army

I have always been at the mercy of madness
and memory
and
now I find myself obliged
by my own interference
into a conversation between myself and myself and myself
and you.

Take this city, this
New York City street tonight. It's raining but
the sideshows and sidewalks are not wet. Yet

it's 1930 and everyone is listening
still
to the Stock Market on Wall Street, 1929

still crashing
like Charles Lindbergh never cleared
by the control towers on Madison Avenue
to land
between the lines,
long ugly lines
of black and white photography people
still
standing at parade unrest,

Disband the Army

still
hugging the streets and corners of an invisible job market.
Work has completely stopped looking for herself

in the Monday morning mirror.

Now, if you will,
turn and flip this photograph
and tell me what you do not see

a sign that says COLORED ONLY WAITING ROOM.
Between the lines, the other upside down,
a sign that means NO WHITE LADIES ALLOWED

to see the jazz of me
and Man Ray, half drunk because Man Ray does not drink
because Man Ray is dead as a blue pan.

Surrealism
killed herself on New Year's Eve. Man Ray
had just arrived from New York City and we,

you and I, were not yet born. We were asleep,

too sound to climb up from our dreams of falling
like rain on a night of no rain. Sketches of Spain.

There was no storm,
but we heard thunder in the voices of white gods.
We heard the white falsetto of white angels
singing
like Negroes in a summer hot church room full
of Sunday afternoon fried chicken feathers.

So we danced to the Gospel according to a world between
two fried chicken wars.

Disband the Army

We transformed content into unhurried empty space
allowing
the mystery of the diminished to transform
into the undiminished
revealing

more of her legs than necessary
from my angled drunk perspective. Marvelous
is always beautiful,
but beautiful is never always anything. Take Lee Miller,
legs long as an advertisement for buying a bath tub robe.

The element of Dada surprise, the androgynous appearance
of wearing a woman's coat. The dialogue between

love and her enemy, logical conclusion.
The intimacy between
subject and viewer.

Avant-garde,

the transformation of eroticism into eroticism. Lee Miller,

her eyes
her lips
her legs
her white face whiter than the white
between white and white.

Lee Miller, wearing nothing
but a black dress

and my imagination. Now

imagine me, incomplete as three quarters of a full moon,

walking sideways into a night of no rain. Sketches of Spain.

The avenues listen, but no one hears the question.
What is a moment of existentialism
doing among moments of surrealism?

Realism, the street man said, is eating in a café
and not having the time or the money to pay
the truck-stop waitress for her sweet
"Honey what else can I get you"
voice.

Surrealism, the street man said, is the way yellow cabs
and yellow cars and yellow cow butter blur
the lines of life. I have no life,

and Man Ray is dead as a blue pan. All of this is nothing
more than

Disband the Army

a postscript on a post-war postcard
mailed from post Paris
found on the floor of the Saturday Evening Post
office
explaining why I no longer live
in the letters
I no longer write
to the woman I no longer love.

The second time I killed myself,
I killed myself to live,
the first time to die,
the third time, I will spare you

if you will consent to listen
to the way Lee Miller walks across the marble floor
of a cheap motel

returning like a street girl
flamboyant blonde, flamboyant brunette,
woman of thirty years,
the fugitive blue character of escaped love.
So

Disband the Army

Lee Miller and I
had breakfast in topcoats and fur
on the restaurant cover
of a Norman Rockwell magazine cover.

Memory has the right to edit
the time of day, but not the time of year.
It was too cold for tears.

With words we danced over wine that was blue.
The coffee black darkness lifted the veil and we talked
in disconnected monologue
scripted as dialogue.

I said, *The Assassin threatened.*

She said, *Hand Catching a Bird.*

I said, *The Feast of Silk.*

She said, *Burnt Bridges.*

I said, *The Start of a Chestnut Tree.*

She said, *Say Two Words.*

I said, *Invisible Object.*

She said, *Say Two Words.*

I said, *Aphrodisiac Jacket.*

She said, *Say Two Words.*

I said, *The End.*

We both said, *Salvador Dali and Frida Kahlo*
are not the same person. Then

God spoke, and I spelled His name wrong but not backwards.
Still He slapped me back
into the middle of the day after yesterday.

Disband the Army

Breakfast in fur moved over.
Love escaped in the refill of a wine blue glass
but not before the night before …

before I painted a new frame
around the portrait of Lee Miller.
Man Ray got mad. Sad

can only be happy out of context. So
out of context I painted a frame
too fragile to hold onto my fragile self-reflection
of myself.

The next morning love escaped
from a room without a door.

Escaped love,
the fugitive blue color of blue.

The trick of optics
and light. Dead black light hidden by this night of no rain.
Sketches of Spain.

All along it had been
without being. The streets are not
still,
I am soaking wet. I know all

water is holy, still blind thirst cannot be quenched

Disband the Army

because the eye cannot hear
as well as the ear can see. Therefore
before you decide,
the question automatically composes itself
then poses itself to you.

Do you believe in red
the way red believes in the color red?

This is 1930. This is New York City.
There is nothing left to believe in.

This is a photograph taken without a lens.

Look into the black basic black box. This is what you see.

Herbert Hoover is the architect. He built this city of ruins.
Hoover Times is not a newspaper reporter.
He's a one story structure told too many times
in too many different ways to ever …

But Cool Calvin Coolidge is still trying to figure out

the relationship between the State of the Union

and the state where he believes he was born.

November refuses to remember 1929. I do not blame her,
she didn't know she was pregnant.
October that year was born a black baby boy. Nothing
but no luck at all.

Depression is Art Deco. Picasso is pink.
The big woman is blonde.
Dorothy Parker is in town.
There's a party on the third floor.
Picasso is pink. Depression is Art Deco.

Henri Ford is in France
painting all cars French fried black.

Roosevelt is still young, though FDR never was
wrong
is always partly right even if
wrong
is completely wrong. Louis Armstrong
blowing the same ole song, improvising

the possible impossibility of possibility.

Walker Evans is walking across Alabama
wearing nothing but a pair khaki shorts
with a camera
around his neck, eating

grapes and drinking wraths of two-for-a-dime-wine,
shooting in black and white,
snapshots of niggers and soda boy crackers
sitting on the back porch of America
falling in love with the color of white girls.

This is what I see, forgive me
for looking like I just woke up. Forgive

me for the problems caked in my eyes. I'm too tired
to see what I've already seen. Forgive me

for wearing my public hat in this unpublic place.
Forgive me for the color,
I won't mention my face. Choice chooses
itself every time.

Disband the Army

Forgive me for sleeping on a park bench
in the middle of the street.
I was trying to escape the principles
of reality.

Forgive me for cutting the deserted branches
from the dreamer's tree. I wanted you to see

the other side of where we sleep. "After me,"

I said to Lee Miller, "sleep." Surrealism
killed herself in Paris on New Year's Eve
in New York City. Gertrude Stein attended the funeral, solo.
Where is Alice, where can Alice "B."?
"A rose is a rose is a rose is a rose," Gertrude whispered
to me as she was leaving. I left with Lee Miller

on my mind and in my pocketbook. Memory
has the right to edit. The truth
is not true.
Like René Magritte
who painted a print of a tobacco pipe
and titled his pipe "This is Not a Pipe,"

this is not a page, and I am not a poem or a poet,
and everything that I've said to you
in these last three hours
means
absolutely nothing.

Designated by these words, if I may offer

pure evidence,
is nothing but an illusion

of a surrealist woman of thirty years,
and me and Man Ray half drunk,
because Man Ray does not drink
because Man Ray is dead as a blue pan of water

in this street, in this year of bad weather wine
and beautiful snow birds
that do not discriminate. They shit on everything
except statues. And

here I stand in the middle of everything I forgot to say
with absolutely nothing on my mind but
how to appear handsome to a woman in the street
and you.

What about you?
I haven't forgotten about you.

You do not exist unless
the third typist decided to type your name
onto the pages of that book of nothing
but
names and telephone numbers.

Do not be afraid.
Do not worry your pretty smile thin.
I have no intentions
of calling you, but
what I like about you
is you
do not forgive.

TWO

DRY WEATHER WARS
ZOO STORIED
INTO
A
DESERT SAND BOX

THE NIGHT BEFORE CHRISTMAS:

A Sister's Song of Praise for Her Two Little Brothers
Playing Marbles on a Persian Rug
— Iraq, March 17, 2003 (just before midnight)

Even now with my soft palms placed flat
against a sweating windless window
I see, still, the beauty of Baghdad,
my holy city of holy nights.

I see the sway of my loose skirt
caught
in breeze consistent with the lack of
detectable movement. I see stars
in a sky without
stars, only eyes that see everything.

It is as dark as dark gets on this, the night before
Illumination, and nothing is

moving except the dogs
of late winter. Tomorrow morning, quite early,

the desert boots of another man without a name,
named by another name, will come marching in

for holy holiday breakfast, breaking down
all doors yellow,
looking for what
hides

when one knows not
what one seeks.
Tall, dark, ugly, imposing, impending

another Desert Storm sand rain storm rain of
total confusion will amass its forces then fuse
into illuminated illusion

that all can never be well without according to …

Precautions,

we do not believe I comes before E except after
wait and see.
We have no stockpiles to stock and pile
up against the shaking hearts of this city destroyed
like Troy

too many warlords and war years before
the sacred eyes of what Christ and what Christmas
morning. Tonight everything
is
waiting for God not Godot.

The dishes in the kitchen sink are clean.
The tile designed floor, mopped and swept.
The hallway closet doors are shut.
Cockroaches who never sleep, tonight are asleep
on top of a refrigerator who has forgotten
her hum. We

have no electrical power. Light
in a kerosene lamp is damp and dark. Candles
on the mantel flicker faintly between

life and death and forgiveness, melting unkindly into
themselves as candles always do. My father sits

still as a leather stone chair in a long yellow room. My mother

is making green tea for the whole world. My little brothers
play marbles on a Persian rug of reason, completely,
almost
in the dark. They have little idea of the makeup of tea bags.
I am standing.

I am a woman at the window, wondering
as I look out at my 17-year-old life, wondering
what this Christmas will bring
tomorrow morning

to the good children of Baghdad.
All now is calm
against the backdrop black
of an unsuspecting black night sky
line
full of good gray brick buildings asleep
not knowing

the implications of democracy imposed.
Tomorrow they, the good and the gray, will explode
and implode into themselves without
ever realizing that falcons and
eagles and hawks and U.S. fighter jets are all birds
of prey.

What will the newspapers say, tomorrow?

What about the children? My little brothers, 7 and 8,
caught completely, in the formations of marbles.

Each lies completely straight across
an angled Angelic Islamic Arabic life
and shoot completely straight
into a future of tangled up words
and war. Tomorrow morning will be a box

gift wrapped and warped in stars and stripes
and dropped
like rain from an unforgiving dead sky. My father

at this moment
is watching the designs on yellow wallpaper.

The windless blue curtains are not moving
at all. The sad yellow table
is curled up in the sad yellow corner
of its own sad yellow life. The front door

is locked and bolted and looking
back at me. The toilet, I can hear it,
is running away, wasting precious desert water.

Outside,
the night has only starless eyes, and the moon
must be dead by now.
I don't see her anywhere. I have my time of month.
I can feel the flow
of my own blood rushing and

running down my legs into the streets
of my Baghdad tomorrow morning quite early.

The children of dead mothers will not forget.

My little brothers, silent now. Nothing
but the cracking hard sound of marbles
colliding with life. The streets and sidewalks, too,

are quiet but not overly so.
We've been through the impending before.
Somewhere

somebody
not so far away is playing soft sweet Spanish music.
What a night to be in Barcelona. A sitar or a guitar?
I refuse to decide
the color of this war without color.

Tonight is a bull fight, a preemptive party
in celebration of a preemptive air strike.

I am a matador without a veil. I am a woman.
I, now, see clearly why
some of us are different, why
some of us are dead, why
some of us see red, why
some of us are
quiet and still as my father. I see clearly

Conflict and her twin sister, Contradiction,
both worn,
battle born Bible verses from the Book of
Deception.
Tomorrow

at the perfect moment, at the perfect drop of
a poetic yellow pencil, the small gods of stars

and stripes and Baghdad, player without pipes,

will drop small boxes of hard candy
into the small hands of small children

and each small god
will know each small child
by name just as each small child will know
his name,

George Washington.

You may not ask, but, no, I do not want to be Miss America.

I am an insecure 17-year-old insurgent looking out
from a windless window on this night of no
redemption.

We didn't blow up the World Trade Center.
We didn't blow up anything. We only blow like sand
in this desert life. Like anyone, we wake, then go.

We know, we all know that
he and him and him and he are
both, just as Texas as the city of
Houston, Texas,
both, just as British as British Petroleum,
both, just as cruel as crude black oil
flowing
through the veins of a pipeline that runs
directly
from Baghdad to your Japanese SUV
sitting

quite quietly in your front yard driveway
tonight. A paper thin pipeline designed by design.

What crime did the babies who will die tomorrow
commit? You say
we make bombs in milk factories. Do you
make bombs in milk factories? You say

we house militias in elementary schools. You say
we have weapons to destroy the masses. Now

you tell me who will be mass destroyed tomorrow.
You say
you have facts and conclusions
based on solid intelligence. You say

the ghost of Osama sleeps homeless on the steps
of every church in Baghdad, in the doorway
of every mosque in Fallujah. Solid intelligence,

facts and conclusions?
What crime

did my little brothers, lost in the play of dark marbles,
commit?
What crime

did my mother commit? She only wants
to give to this world
a cup of hot green tea.
What crime

did my father, still as the chair he sits in, commit?
You say
you have facts and conclusions based on solid intelligence.

I'll tell you what's solid. At this moment
there's a taxi downstairs, solid white, blowing
a solid brass trumpet, echoing
into this, a solid black night of

flawlessly solid literary construction with solid
haunting themes and solid metaphors that keep
solid
the relation between
solid white baby milk and solid white milk factories
and the dropping of
hard solid candy for the children of
Baghdad.

The weather forecast
has been set to correspond exactly with
the impending
desert dust decorations of Christmas graves,
announcing in a clear to partly cloudy voice,
announcing the arrival of a man wearing
no shoes to cover his oil slicked soul,
announcing the coming

of the planters of flowers of evil. I have never been
to Afghanistan
but I know it is nothing to you but
a field of heroin trees and poppy weeds. And
on this eve of my own destruction, we know
we, too, will be planted

by the shape and shake of jets dropping bird shit
disguised as hard candy
for the children
running and playing and dancing
and laughing and
then

exploding

quite vividly into the face of a couch
as far away as Santa Fe, New Mexico,
color television, wide screen, narrow minded
CNN,
around the world in 30 slanted minutes. Listen,

you say you have facts and conclusions based on
solid intelligence.

Did your intelligent CIA tell you?

Did you intelligent FBI tell you?

Did your intelligent Secretary of Offense tell you?

Did some intelligent nobodies tell you, Mr. George
Washington,
that milk in milk factories in Baghdad is milk?

Did your intelligent female National Security Advisor
advise you,
Mr. President, that you are not God?

Solid intelligence?
Make no mistake, we know.

Sure
tomorrow dead Iraqi men will carry dead Iraqi women
through the dead streets of Baghdad.

Sure
Iraqi mothers, like my mother, will make green tea
for the dead sad dead feelings of this war-torn city.

Sure
the Iraqi old will die and be dead without the dignity
they barely had anyway.

Sure
we will die quicker than we can dig, and our graves
will be mass Christmas music graves. But

you be sure, Mr. and Mrs. George and Martha,
that we are not afraid of your Virginia Woolf. Be sure
that 8,000, 9,000, 10,000 miles away from this night,
this day, this land

of dead sand,
a man will knock solid on your mid-morning door
and, he, this man with no name,
in the solid voice of no good reason, will announce,

"The U. S. Army and the Joint Chiefs of Staff regretfully
inform
you that …
Johnny can't read because Johnny is dead

from a slip and a fall
on the crude cruelness of an oil leak in your own driveway.
Time of death: Central Standard Oil Time."

And
Johnny's other life, his other wife, his next of kin, a needle
found rusted in Opium City, Afghanistan. I've never been,
but I know

a man with a hole in his soul vowed revenge
for his father's failed attempt to conquer the crude
sands of time, 13 years solidly removed

from the slow ticking moments
upon which I now stand, shaking, looking out
from a windless window, long yellow room.

I was 4 years old then
when the good gray Christmas jets came
and tore out the pages of my Christmas coloring book.

Now again sadly on this, the Eve of Invasion,
I am forced, with no such glue,
to glue back the chapters of this book I now write
with no designed cover to cover the things that cover
nothing
but my tears and my sand, storming beneath the silence of
this,
my last page.

LATE FOR SCHOOL

A Photograph: An Israeli Settler Protects His Daughter during an Attack on the Road Linking the Crossing Between ...

God is an ugly man this morning, slinging down thunder
from a sky, perfect Palestinian blue.

The chariot horses of Ariel are descending down
upon the ash laden aisles of Yasser. Sonic, a voice

by no other name, too loud to describe, a bomb,

a BOOM, a rocket standing ovation rocks
and rolls this daybreak into parts too unevenly divided
to play on a stage this small in this Holy state of ...

Confusion.

I cover my ears and hear with my heart. Morning

is angry at the sky and as sweet as laughter can sometimes be, she
does not smile down upon these streets where children have forgotten

the sweet joy of play.
Where they fall, the children stay. Ordinary,
another cruel angel named Monday. Me and my father covered
in the crimes of white ash, look out from beneath

a homemade street-side table. From here the world is flat. Horrible
is not as horrible as this horror. Even I struggle to believe

the ghost of my mother has come again, disguised again
in the voice of a pretty boy from Memphis of all places, Tennessee.
My mother was 31. Elvis was her song, her soul,
her everything

now rocked and rolled up inside memories of Mother,
a brown moment hiding in plumes of godless brown smoke.

I don't understand. My father never tried to hear her music.
Maybe she was born on the day Elvis died, or maybe
Elvis died on the day she was born. Believe what you will.
Maybe all mothers

are born and die on Monday, the same day. Believe what
you will, nothing is beside, beyond, or behind this point
I make, but maybe

all bombs are rock 'n' roll suicide, a tragic, magic
no carpet red concert, free in Central Park, Palestine.
I'm a girl. I'm Jewish.
What do I know except this is my homeland and

here we have come to expect the expected ghost of my mother
dressed as a pretty boy from Memphis of all places, Tennessee
rocking the streets of this place without a face unscarred.

Will she protect me and my father, or will she bury us
in the grave of her own destruction?
Delusion?
This I do not know. I know only what I see,

and I see a blaze,
a man runs red into the blue flames of this Beale street. I am

screaming, "Mother is this the rock 'n' roll you loved?"
My father covers my voice. Still I choke,

godless brown smoke, I choke to understand what
really propels a rocket propelled grenade,

American made.
Horror

must be a stationary fool to believe
homemade bombs have no taste at all. Call it bitter,
call it sweet in the street of Holy Koran. We

eat what we plant. Settlements and settlements and settlements
and shacks and newspaper stacks all fall and burn in-
to the lyric of this *Do not love me tender* song. Elvis.

Another explosion, another rock rolls and
fails
to explain

the meaning of my mother's memory except to say
"It's a helluva time to be thinking about the color
of blue shoes. Reporters dance in as they dash out to report,
slanted, what they report, "The King Ain't Dead."

I am screaming. I, too, am slanted. I am a schoolgirl
on a school day, drunk as the unjoy
of this black velvet morning. Panicked

people clamber over and behind what's left standing.
A white Cadillac, beaten up and ugly as this morning's God,
engulfed

in the cruel blue smell of smoke, waits
to explode into a drum solo

while
Elvis, back stage, changes into that black haunting black leather
jacket, a 1969 comeback Israeli, comeback to the motherland
tour.
My mother, wearing boy's clothes, drifts
in and out, godless brown smoke. I lift every one of my voices
and sing "That's Alright Mama,"

as the roar of planes dances
and dives just above my head in a now black crazy sky.
I don't wanna die.
I am 13.

My mother was 31. My father's black beard, longer than my hair,
fails to muffle the melody of these uneasy moments

and minutes, mad at each other for being forced to tick
and tock in the same clock,
in the same settlement on the West Bank of nowhere safe.

Now
sound the bell.
In 5 minutes it will be 5 minutes after 8,
and I will be late for school.

One half of one second away from my ear,
I can smell my father's fear
fighting
the refrain "Don't step on my blue shoes,
don't step on my fucking blue shoes." I talk like I talk

’cause I live like I live.

Half a second the other way,

blasted,
a vegetable stand recognizes itself as nothing more than
a thing for other things to be placed upon and leaves it at that,

three legs, broken, and a tabletop headache.

Blitzed,
cucumbers split straight up the middle,
front and center, a shaking stage, too small to contain it all.
Tomatoes,
tomatoes, tomatoes everywhere,
blown easily into a total eclipse,
godless brown smoke. Lettuce, a beautiful head,

tossed
to a perfect breakfast salad, dressed in the yellow run
of yellow chicken eggs and eyes.

A man,
his hands, shaking on the ground, detached,
dead, looking up
to find the arms of what God

by what name.
Another man measures
the distance between his left foot and what’s left
of his left shoe,

nothing left suede, nothing left blue. Two

old ladies on bicycles decide to run instead of ride,

suicide,

a bomb
blows the wheels off. Still they, the wheels, go round and round
and round
and rolling, then falling into
the putrid red smell of blood coloring in the hollowed out design
of all roads

leading

to me and my father under this table. This world is flat.
I can't see, godless brown smoke. What map decided
to place this New Jerusalem on top of Old Jerusalem?

What is a strip of Gaza?
What Jesse James robbed the West Bank? Where
is my book bag? I can't feel

my fingers. My father is praying. My mother is drifting
in and out of sacred-unsacred memory. The streets
are yelling.
What are they saying, and who are these
streets talking to?

The birds
even they know the trajectory of this rock
music, loud as the young Palestinian boys throwing stones
at tanks and trunks and armored cars.

This Beale Avenue can talk.

This is Beale Street war.

This is Beale Street life.

This is Beale Street rock 'n' roll.

This is Beale Street routine. A young mother is running carrying a baby carriage. What a helluva time to be born. I talk like this because ...

Damn the Memphis sun and the Memphis shine.

A schoolboy dashes, direction insane. He has no lunch box. Maybe he forgot his lunch, or maybe his lunch forgot about him

and a million other boys just like him
all lined up to be shot

eventually. Me,
we grow up too quick in these streets
of godless brown smoke. Where we fall, we stay.

Another shop explodes
the market into chaotic deception. Daylight, confused, fuses
into a morning brown night without the light of a single star.
A bus empty
calmly flips
out a cigarette, lights up the world and smokes
into misunderstanding
us children
too young to buy a pack of American-made Marlboros

for the price of
a day without war. Insane

is the only direction on a broken compass.
Dogs, stray as a slanted newspaper reporter,
undance a tangled up tango
to the music of raw rock market place meat,

blasted
into guitar lick and lyric. No need to read the headlines.

My father's black beard, longer than my hair,
braided into the Bible and laced in 3 thousand years of Jewish
zealotry,

reaches down

tickling the nape of my neck. My skirt with no pockets
into which I have no place to place my shaking hands.

Homemade bomb
for breakfast, beneath a homemade table, we eat

what we plant. I am screaming, I am crying, I am laughing
in the face of godless brown smoke. My glasses are not broken.
I am happy. I choke
to understand the dance of this concert.

Gunshots ring out,
splitting the air, piercing my unpierced ears. I am 13. My father
allows no lipstick, no eyeliner, no nothing magic. My mother
was 31.

A sniper across the way
has fallen in love with the rooftop. Bullets shatter windows,
glass falls

in love with itself. I have nothing left. Patterns on my plaid skirt

dead before design, struggle to reclaim the refrain: Nothing
left beyond the ordinary. "14 Minutes in Hell" is the name

of this novel, and I'm reading every word twice
for the third time when

suddenly then and without audible warning,

out of the cruelness, an uneven easy breeze struts in
as plumes,
godless brown smoke,

drifts out in the direction of the Dead Sea.

It's my mother taking with her, the dogs of rock 'n' roll.

The sky, it, refuses to cry. "Why" is not a simple word.
The red ants crawling
up my leg have no idea I, too, am looking
for a crumb in this life.

Up from under the table, me and my father,
we stand and look out

into the long face of a world, no longer flat
now spinning around again

as silence slips slowly past, pushing aside what's left,
godless brown smoke.

Minutes and moments for a moment
seem no longer mad for being forced to tick and tock
in the same clock. Everyone is looking at everyone else.

Death
takes a death count and settles on a fatal uncaring number.

The street changes back from unholy brown to
uncrazy blue and breathes
forgiveness. The white ash apologizes to my father's black beard,

longer than my hair.
Untouched,
a cup of broccoli winks at me
as if to say, "This life goes on, my little Jewish one."
I don't believe
in broccoli. Crowds, insane
just minutes ago, now go almost as if nothing happened.
A man,
a donkey
and a donkey cart almost calmly cart away the remains
of the last Monday in May,
a holiday in Memphis of all places, Tennessee.

My broken watch will be right exactly two times
again tomorrow.

Almost 8:30 now I suppose, I really didn't want to go
to early morning math, anyway.

The last of the brown smoke dissipates as finally

"Elvis Aaron Presley has left this building,"

that haunting black

black leather jacket,
black leather pants,

white Graceland Memphis
white Cadillac,

insane blue
blue suede shoes,
not worn at all.

The curtain can find no reason to call

and I, 13 years old,

for the first time in my life, am able to see
clearly what
Mama saw
in the man who still shakes the whole world
from time to time.

THREE

CAROLINA STORMS
DISGUISED
BY
THE BACKDROP
OF
TWO
EAST COAST HURRICANES

STORM NAMED EARL

Wilmington, North Carolina

Years later, a storm named Earl
would come swinging wind across
this city named in 1730
for the Earl of Wilmington.

We called them storms then.
When I was a kid, hurricanes
were named for girls, pretty girls
like Hazel and Juanita.

Every year of those growing up years,
rain, heavy as angry air pounded
and pushed September into October,

into the first few cold days
of sad November. I remember
garbage cans and lids, effortlessly,
flying down the street. Sometimes

drifting like dirty sheets of white
school boy, notebook paper,
beating down the coastline
of my seaport, pirate town.

Wind the size of titanic waves
bounced the city farther
and farther inland. Outlets
and inlets traded places

on the fear laden faces of real estate
beach front property

ownership. But seasons here, change
as everywhere, I suppose.

Blue crab catching season came in
mid July. Oyster season always came in
time to celebrate the thanks of giving.

You had to be careful driving at night
during deer hunting season
and nigger (known as coon) season
was year round.

In this city where, even today,
Niggerhead Road still haunts
the white center line, I came to love

the river sounds of the Cape Fear.
Catfish big as baby sharks
used to bite off headlines of newspapers
used to wrap up fish stories.

Headlines like, *Negro boy arrested*
for loitering around and about
the New Hanover County Library.

I spent 29 and ½ days waiting
for my social status number
to be verified so I could check out
a 75-cent paperback book.

I never returned it. Precisely
what they were afraid of. I
proved the headlines right

every night when forecasters

plotted the approach of another
impending storm. White people
would board up their windows
with ply board,

mask their faces with tape
across storm front doors, tie down
their yachts and garbage cans,
stock up on flashlight batteries

and perishables, and pray
that all would be saved.

We never did any of this.
The storm was just another god,

and if he wanted to come
into our home, we would let him,
just as we
let the downtown sign-painting god
hang COLORED WAITING ROOM signs

around our necks, just as
we let the bus-driving god direct
us to sit in the rear, just as

we let the restaurant god tell us
not to come in here, just as
we let the water-fountain god offer
to us the coolest drink of water

on any Carolina hot summer day.
I can still hear my grandmamma
saying: "If all we had to worry
about were storms ..."

Years later a storm named Earl
would come, and the black people would
tape up their own windows, but
I would be gone by then.

OF COURSE, THE BROCHURE DOESN'T MENTION MRS. ABBOT

St. Simon's Island, Georgia

The tired, dark people here say when
a hurricane stretches and reaches

Category #3, sometimes the ocean
comes up to Ocean Boulevard, but

the fish do not come to shop
at the Gates of St. Simon's. Today

is Sunday morning, and I'm biking
along Lord Avenue.

How religious can I get without
calling myself to preach the gospel
according to Luke? Everyone

speaks, this morning, to me,
the happy brown stranger in town

wearing a tan fishing hat with hooks

tucked into the science of not catching,
but at the same moment
catching the Sunday slow morning

ambience

like stained blue church window glass

here in this town where hurricanes

can rearrange the cityscape

in a moment, in the fall of any
given year. I, myself, give in

to the straight street level
divide of this fishing village world.

On one side of Lord Avenue,

two island black men rake leaves
and adjust my life and their lives
in a Sunday morning beautiful
flower bed. On the other side,

three young white men
and three young white women brake
and adjust their young handle bar grips

on brightly colored bicycles, preparing

a Sunday morning ride wide into
the *High Tide Guide* of St. Simon's

Island. They know Mullet Bay
is on the way to vacation heaven.

At St. Simon's United Methodist Church,
there's a statement: "Visitors Expected"

and a question, "Are you from Alaska?"
No, I go unannounced

deeper into the low country smell
of Sunday morning
black island coffee. Look at me

walking now and talking to myself
and to the air beneath the horizon
of Spanish-moss-draped oak trees.

The tired, dark people here say

some of the oak trees look back,
actually back at you when you
are not looking back at them.

The tired, dark people here
call them the Spirit-of-looking-back-
trees. Sunday

morning on Lord Knows What
Avenue Now. How religious

can I get without calling myself
to preach the gospel
according to John?

My wife and daughter
in our rented room, still, I imagine,
asleep in pajamas and dreams

of Sunday morning sunshine
yellow and, me reading the sea

island village life
like Sunday morning news.

Maybe I'll take a photograph
and make myself out to be Kodak
Harrison looking

for the right angle to capture
the composition
of Mrs. Abbot sitting quietly
on her Sunday morning porch

dressed quite church like.
She's colored native brown
in a coloring people island book.

She was born here
when the coloring people owned
every dirt road in the village.

"The whole island used to be colored
except," she tells me, "but now …"
And she needs to say no more

about Hazel's Café, still standing
since she was a child, dancing

around a soul food table full
of fried chicken

and collard greens, grown
and raised right in the back yard.

At seventy years old, she
fondly remembers playing

"Simon Says,"
in dirt road front yards before
the legendary white horse came
running down the beach,
thundering up clouds that became
hotel after hotel after hotel.

This was before, she remembers,
roads became streets,

before "Point of Interest"
and "Things To Do" were highlighted
in the *High Tide Guide.*

Before it was necessary
to place a street sign on Lord Avenue,
the tired, dark people knew

the color of Sunday morning
sacred brown crayon. She,
Mrs. Abbot, wears a hat to service today.

I tip mine, and walk on by, in the direction
of a dead end street sign to see
if the road really ends.

FOUR

BLACK BOYS IN A SUPERMARKET IN CALIFORNIA

A SUPERMARKET IN CALIFORNIA

for Allen Ginsberg
(The other king of the dharma bums)

"Clean up on Aisle 6. Kathy, to your register please."
Fresh bread is not always fresh. Fresh fish, catfish,
swordfish. Sharks don't eat lawyers. Fresh eggs
by the dozen or by the half,

and I'm half crazy to be in love with my sectioned-off life.
What kind of knife cuts a man in the middle of a rainstorm?

The night is new, and time is young,
and I'm half tasting the wild
sweet smell of concord grapes.

I am walking into the slow praise of walking. My shoes
are the same color as wearing no shoes.
The Saturday night blues

of being blue as you-know-who. Big black Sweet Mama
crying tonight in her big blue everyday room.

Fresh salmon, fresh shrimp, farm-raised like goats
and cow milk, 100 percent lactose free. Kathy is a pretty frown
in a grocery store circus, a walking red lipstick trick

over things that do not matter. E does not equal MC square
over there in the checkout line.
Kathy, a real California Pacific Standard charm.
Her face,
brief as an empty briefcase.
Kathy has a head full of red crazy whitegirl hair.

Everything is everywhere,
California calendar girls, granola boys and girls,
and the bad girls
of the ballet and aisle after aisle after aisle
of supermarket super models
catwalking on a runway, landing right on schedule
before takeoff. This plane is full and

whoever's steering this ship must be drunk.
It's midnight bright

and LAX is flying out of context in this morning of
sad confusion in the made up constellation
of starclouds and grocery store crowds.
Confucius was wrong.

The supermarket superman only thinks he can fly.
The other eye
of the surveillance camera is a super market zealot,
trained in super fashion to follow only the way pants hang
low on young black boys, 4 of them.

4 different colors of a pair of underwear. They don't care
about the way size fits into the attitude of being born to die
in the crowded, vacant streets of America.

4 black boys.
So easily the blind camera boy forgets
who the real robbers in America are.
So easily the blind camera boy forgets
the privilege of riding in the front seat, denied.
So easily the blind camera boy forgets
the consequence of life sacrificed young.

4 black boys.
Just as easily they forget that they have forgotten
what Sweet Mama sent them to the store to forget.

I can stand here all night weighing
and re-weighing the same
head of cabbage on this scale of life. What is the relationship

between wearing pants slung down too low
and having no father
to speak of? What is the relationship between riding all day

in a too loud music hoochie mobile and having no father
to speak of? What is the relationship
between showing no respect

and having no father to respect?
What is the difference between no direction
and no direction?

I can stay in the corner of this supermarket all night,
the weight of a head of cabbage refuses to change
the price we pay.
Young black boys are the most expensive people in America.

4 black boys, sons of fake fathers too cool to name.
Fake fathers, fake ID. God knows Sweet Mama knows exactly
who and why Cool Street gives birth to the coolest
fake

as a rubber rattlesnake crawling up and overlooking
the midnight cooking lady cooking up midnight samples
on Aisle 15 between the cleaning products,

and the cleaning products,

4 black boys playing golf on the kosher food aisle while
the blind camera boy waits, looking intently through
his Ronald Reagan California sunglasses.

America does not steal the shoe. America steals the box,
Fort Knox, magic kingdom viridian,
off-key colored green notes and other denominations.
What church do you not go to, and who is Harry Houdini
anyway?

And how did he get out of that triple locked blue steel iron box
life? This American Life,
filleted to fit into the big back pockets of George Washington
and Andrew Jackson's driveway, gateway, causeway, anyway

except the right way. We all look. The meat cutter keeps cutting
fresh meat. The beer aisle is a street tonight.

Hey, Allen Ginsberg, what ya doing watching them
grocery boys?

Zoom in blind camera boy, the honey thief
is making a God-shaped hole and filling her pockets
with a pear and a peach, and each of us refuse to see that

Rainy Night in Georgia is the wrong sad song to be playing
on the cat food aisle tonight. Cat walk, supermodel or
Supertramp, *Breakfast in America* is a question: "What is a grit
and how do you shoot it?"

I am caught in the solid gaze of my own stare. Looking

everywhere
supermarket supersomething
supernormal and superficial.

Something
about being in here in this store gives an odd flat shape to a world
I know is round.

I'm checking labels.
How many proteins in a can of Norwegian sardines?

The Please-Sell-By-Date slides up and into the sleeve
of what I no longer believe. A single can of Pork 'n' Beans seems
the only one to notice that I'm a lonely man tonight.

Where does the attitude of rain come from? Crying season
is the fifth season in California tonight in this grocery store.
Fire season is the fourth.

The black boys are drumming in the toy section.
The blind camera boy
is blind, still he hums along. Rap music is hard
to wrap in old newspaper.
This is a story
that takes 3 weeks to tell. I'm gonna try to get out
of this store in 21 minutes.

Wearing a bow tie at a careless slant,
an old-white-professor-looking man is drinking Bud Light
right outta the case, relaxed and easy as a football game,

watching Tennessee college boys on game day afternoon,
the third Saturday in October. Face red, eyes red as

Crimson low Tide, Alabama. George Wallace

is buried next to the back door to a black church on Side Street
next to the watermelon aisle. The camera is watching

everything but only sees 4 black boys playing
soccer in Spain on the olive tree aisle, while

up on Beer Street, Professor Don't Care doesn't care.
He's opening another Bud Light. It's midnight and

the moon is mad because it's raining in crying town.
The shopping midnight secretaries are typing
on computers until all computers drop dead out of the sky.

The landscape is littered with tracked-in cigarette butts
and broken hearts.
The always Mexican janitor man is taking his time,
sweeping up heartbreaks and pain
on the headache and pain medication over-the-counter aisle.

There's a frosty silence to this rude rhythm. Everybody
is talking
to somebody on a cell phone.
Soaps and operas play out on a
midnight game board.

I am as guilty as many on some nights,
but tonight
no one wants to know where I am. What kind of knife

cuts a man into parts in the middle of a rainstorm?

The trade of the heartbreak trick. Sam Walton is an illusionist.
The god-like tracks of a trickster coming to a theater
very close to you. The plot:

The supermarket monster eats Mom and Pop. Should've built
a brick store front. Too late to live on Main Street now.
The supermarket super thinker thinks twice without

any thoughtful acknowledgment of his own thinking.

The professor is drunk by now and still drinking out loud
in plain wide open view, clear as segregation in America.

The taco section next to the neckbone section next
to the prime rib section next
to the next section
next
to the fully loaded semi-automatic semi-dirty
magazine erection section next
to the election section.

Who did you vote for? Did you forget?
November was the month that shot John Kennedy.

Professor Don't Care doesn't want to know.
The king is in a bottle of beer. It's hot in here, but

attitude in this place is cold. Camera number 1

angle number 2, 4 black boys in baggy pants

slung down too low in the sto
not store

sto
with less than mo
not more
mo
zero
gotta go
catch a ho
not whore
a ho
or a you know
what
gangsta style.

Meanwhile,
their future does not know which way to go.
To the Army or prison
football college or prison
basketball USC or prison
4 choices for 4 black boys.

Turn up the rap music, maestro.
Turn it up loud enough to shake
the car three doors down.

F U C K the C H I P and the L A P D
and all ya'll ain't nothing to me,
and yes we use double negatives
cuz
we is double dangerous. 4 black boys speak.

Rap music is hard
to wrap up in old newspaper.

The blind camera is blind. Weapons of mass destruction
not found.
The soldier never takes his uniform off.
Roxy and Boxy are twin seeing-eye bulldogs.

Hey, Allen Ginsberg,

what ya doing over there watching them grocery bag
boys.

The supermarket supermodels huddle in the super salad
section

talking about the weight of a single carbohydrate. "Kathy,
to your register, please." "Someone from management
to the service desk, please."

Bad girls of the ballet shopping for a light
brown handy man. Dare repeat repair
for a promise and a please. The standing
at-attention soldier boy stands now at-ease.

Professor Don't Care doesn't care
one way or the other way.

In this world of pork chop mannerism, and commotion,
Chop Suey is in a case all by herself.

This is a movie, and it's rated LA triple X, and
we've been cleared. We're number one for takeoff even if
this plane never leaves the runway. America
is not beautiful. Uncle Sam Walton is an illusionist.

A tree for a tree. Cut down one tree, then cut down another
tree because you cut the first tree. Who needs trees
when we can live in an apartment complex
called and named Whispering Pines and Piney Woods.

This is a story
that takes 3 weeks to tell, I'm gonna try to get out
of this store in 21 minutes.

10 minutes to go, and I have a total of 2 items in my cart,
my umbrella and my list of shopping confusion.

Confucius was wrong.
The supermarket superman only thinks he can
fly like an airplane.

It's a hard train that trains a blind camera boy
to train only on 4 black boys dancing to the hip hop
bebop beat of having a good time,
wearing pants way too big,

made way too far away in Shanghai
by children way too poor to afford the football
numbers on the backs of football jerseys.

Number 81 TO, Number 81 TO

Number 81 TO, and Number 81 TO.

Thomas Overstocked takes a time out,

but time is already out for 4 black boys

at a supermarket in California.

LAX laid out flat in the end zone.

The Philadelphia Eagle has landed without
torching or touching the ground.

A touchdown with no extra point.

No kicker can see the uprights
from 75 yards out. "Chemical spill
on the Clorox aisle." " 436 on Aisle Number 6."

"Kathy to your register, please."

"137 on Aisle Number 7."

3 black boys and a black boy

throwing a football.

Call the police.

Third and nine on their own 5 yard line.

3 black boys and a black boy

call a shotgun play.

It's only the third quarter, and

I apologize to you my dear audience

for making this night so long, but

a long night cannot be anything but long.

I don't care
what the newspaper people say.
USA today is a lie
that you can beg, borrow, steal, or buy
for 75 cents. 50 cents was last year. Inflation
is telling a woman you love her when you don't
know that a 25-cent jump in the price of
a newspaper is a 50 percent increase
in the decrease of truth. Uncle Sam
doesn't give a damn

about Mom and Pop and their place

that used to be on the corner
where all of us used to sit, laugh, and eat
hamburgers with fries, drinking a cherry Coke.

Now
whole families shopping at night, shopping
for whole families
shopping at night. Carts full of nothing but
chili peppers.

It's hot in here with an overcast cool attitude.

Hey, Allen Ginsberg,

what ya doing over there watching them grocery bag
boys?

Professor Don't Care is making a baloney sandwich.

The meat cutter's buzzer rings.

How thin can you cut a thin steak? That old black lady
came to LA 40 years ago, now
she wants to feed the idea of steak
to as many people as she can.

A man, white as his business button-down
white shirt carries the son
of whom he calls "his bitch," walking
measurable paces behind the both of them.

Tonight is a broken heart with a hangover
headache.

And the time of the night refuses to care.
Professor Don't
open that jar of mayonnaise. The black boys,
two riding in two carts, two pushing two carts
too fast for this section of Bread Street.

An old black man wearing homeless clothes
pays for his homeless life
with pennies for a single can of creamed corn.

An impatient checkout line counts along with Kathy,

37 California pennies plus a 9 percent California tax
on a single can of creamed corn
for an old black man wearing homeless clothes.

Who knows
why Chop Suey is in a case by herself.

Supermarket supermodels, illegible smiles, illegal
up and down the long streets of superstitious aisles.

Wonder woman and Super girl on the cover
of every *Vogue* magazine. Something about being

in this store gives an odd flat shape to a world
I know is round. The barn dance fiddle plays on

playing a Charlie Daniels, Jack Daniels' *Devil*
Went Down to Georgia smoking fiddle song. Play
it, Charlie Boy til that thing catches on fire and

burns this place down to the ground. Now
let Miles Davis play some crying blue

midnight morning blues, sad and weeping
into the section of non-toys and 4 black boys
each thinking solo. Each does not know
that tomorrow may never come crawling
as a promise
packaged as a Philadelphia 76er. Allen I.,
the king of the crossover dribble.

Who
will tell them
in a letter mailed by nobody from Nowhere,

North Carolina or North Dakota?

4 black boys in a world too loud and too big
for this supermarket world.

Who
will tell them
that dreaming is dangerous?

Who
will tell them
that in America, we vote to tote
what we as a nation can no longer carry?

Who
will tell them
that Abraham Lincoln was shot
in Washington, DC?

Who
will tell them
that Martin Luther King was shot
in Memphis, Tennessee?

Who
will tell them
that John F. Kennedy was shot
in Dallas, Texas?

Who
will tell them
that Robert Francis Kennedy was shot
in Los Angles, California?

Who

will tell them
that Malcolm X was shot
in New York City?

Who
will tell them
that they all were assassinated

by the same assassination assailant?

Abraham, Martin, Malcolm, John and
Bobby Kennedy. Maybe

the supermarket supermodel will tell
somebody something.

Aisle 11, lookout, here comes
Mr. Important walking like he left his footprints
on the moon. "Kathy, to your register, please."

The blind camera boy is asking blind

Miss Maggie Mae for a blind date.
Ray Charles and Stevie Wonder drive to work
in Braille.

No need to see if you can sing like a piano.
Professor Don't Care is still there essentially
in the same spot as a dog named Spot.

"Look Jane." "No, Dick,
I will not
look" anymore at this Henry Miller air-

conditioned nightmare

America. "You look, Dick Nixon,
if you want to see

how water flows through a gate
in New Orleans."

Federal Express and UPS express nothing,
and nothing

is the name of every side street in America
tonight. Outside it's raining, it's wet, but
the eye of the lie is dry as dry ice. Look.
it's Dick Nixon, again, waving goodbye
from the steps of a presidential helicopter

black as the black magic of being
a black voice
in a black backwards baseball cap
yelling across campus,

I went to college without going to class. Kiss my ass.
4 black boys speak.

Black boys born on Trouble Street.

Black boys die on Trouble Street.

Trouble Street, Trouble Street

where was you born?
The tedium of a baffling existence.

Trouble Street, Trouble Street

where was you born?

Play another Muddy Waters song. Trouble Street
answers

I ain't been born again yet. Stanley Boy Slim
Johnson Reed picking on a red guitar
in a blue and white Chicago blues bar.

According to Bob Dylan or Bob Somebody,
a soldier is America's housewife.

According to the price of cigarettes
in this California supermarket,

R. J. Reynolds Tobacco Co. is a Tar Heel
North Carolina University
Carolina sky blue hat
trick full of supermarket supermodels
smoking hot, blue, cool cigarettes.

Tattoos and belly button rings,
skirts shorter than a short hop
to shortstop.

A double take double play.
Low rise jeans tight as
low-low tide on the beach of sacred promise.

Hair, mostly blonde, folded up
in a hurry. Legs

that beg forgiveness. Arrest me
for looking

like I just woke up. Professor Don't Care
doesn't care
which way the sun shines. America
sells toy shotguns
in the supermarket,
then goes to church and

asks God why Jimmy, age 6,
shot Sally, age 7, in the face.
to make her pretty like a movie
star picture he saw on TV.

The soldiers never take
their uniforms off. Mass deconstruction
never found.

The science of night shopping,
whole families shopping
at night trying to budget the price of
a nice leg of lamb. The ice cream man
in every ice cream store playing
that same sweet summertime ice cream song
on the ice cream aisle in a supermarket
in California

while 4 black boys fall in love
with a tired magazine rack white woman
with moving clouds and movie stars
in her sad blue eyes.

Hey, Allen Ginsberg ...

Alone, white, tired ladies shop
at night, alone. Sex in the City,
Channel 18 every weekday night.

It's Saturday and all clocks
are taking a 5 minute cigarette break.

The pleasure of smoking a Newport
or a Marlboro in this airport
is a sign that says "NO"

young black boys allowed
to live too long or too loud.

Alone, black girls shopping
at night, alone. I can tell
by the sad soft sway, if asked,
what they will say.

"My baby's daddy is gone." Maybe,

they will say, "He's in New York,
New Orleans,
New Mexico,
New London, Connecticut." But

they all will know that I know
and we know
that their babies' daddies
have all been transformed

and transferred to a new level
of maximum security
in a place called New Nowhere, Virginia.

Keep America Safe
is a bumper sticker
slapped onto an old Volvo station wagon.

Keep America Safe. "That's Allstate's stand."

The purpose of a prison is to keep it full.
Stocked
like the stock boy (man), black, on Aisle 17,
blue as a blues recording, recording
the history of Bessie
Smith in his shirt pocket full of blues.

I can tell by his shoes,
he sings in the church choir.

He loves baseball.
I can tell by the way he slings
empty boxes to the side.

A slider, a curve, and then some
high heat. Strike 3,
sit down.

I can tell
he could easily kill a man.

He has been slicing cardboard boxes
with a box cutter for twenty years now.

Just-looking-around distance away,
a mother is stuffing her blouse
while confessing to the 49th god
of California, "My babies need to eat."

Tiny feet
in a room too big for the small play of
small feet. U C L A, but
I see Watts, the neighborhood, reduced
to the hood of a $29.99,
100% cotton sweatshirt made in a sweat shop
in Ho Chi Minh City,

Vietnam, sold right here in this supermarket
on the next aisle over.

The coffee bean aisle smells like 3 BUCKS
and a STAR over Seattle.

Encased waterproof,
lobster Lilly sleeps with rubber bands
around her arms.

Tofu on the tofu aisle
impatiently waits to be sold to anyone
willing to eat tofu.

Oranges court and count apples.
Only one is allowed to be bad.

A lemon tree stares at me because
my heart is as yellow as Van Gogh tonight.

I am an immigrant
in this California immigrant state
of all triangled affairs.

Immigrant state
and I'm not talking about Jamie

and Jesus

and Hector

and Lopez

and Hernandez

and Ortiz

and Maria

and Fidel

and Cristo

and Jesus Christ, Himself,

slung over the rear view
riding in the same
1967 broke-down, pumped-up Chevrolet
full of chrome.

I'm talking about the relationship
between Hollywood and the elements of
San Joaquin.

The holy and the not so
good, Hollywood.

We should all bury our hearts
at Wounded Knee, then we would see
the ghost of Crazy Horse is not crazy
at all. Love is easy

when you lie. Tonight, this night
could be a Jackson Pollock night
slinging paint
and color everywhere. But
tonight, this night is not
in the mood.

This is an Edward Hopper moment
early in morning rain.

Edward Hopper, oil on canvas,

Pretty Penny 1930.

Hey, Allen Ginberg ...

Edward Hopper, oil on canvas,

The Folked Road, 1934.

"Kathy, to your register, please."

Edward Hopper, watercolor over pencil on paper,

Ranch House, Santa Fe, 1925.

Supermarket supermodels, supernatural.

Edward Hopper, oil on canvas,

Conference at Night, 1941.

4 black boys and a blind camera angle.

Edward Hopper, oil on canvas,

Choy Suey, 1929.

in a case by herself.

Edward Hopper, 1887-1967.

The emotive use of light to light
the psychological distance
between people inhabiting the same space,
a supermarket in California.

With chill in the air, I turn up the collar
of my late October jacket.

The electronic door knows me by name.
Two soldier girls
and a soldier boy exit in step to my steps
in step with the slow praise of walking.

13 time zones west of here
and 11 time zones east
a single grain of sand sits quietly tonight
listening

to the night voice of a desert windstorm
singing soft
a lullaby
to a
supermarket
supermodel
supersoldier,

a 19 year old, little, white girl, from Everywhere,
California.

FIVE

VERSIONS OF THE SHIRT I NOW WEAR

YOUNGER THAN NEIL

for Neil Percival Kenneth Robert Ragland Young
And Crazy Horse (the man and the band)

But this ain't no story 'bout no Johnny Rotten.
This is the history of the shirt I'm wearing. Now wait.
Before I tell you this, I must tell you that

a suitcase only gives the illusion of travel. So
to the always going but

no place people
like us

Thirteen niggers sitting on the back porch
drinking *Kool Aid.*

Winter nights in a bus station are never kind.

There are two zoos in the cool but never sweet
peach tree city of ...
One locates exactly where Things Not To Do Street crosses
Things Already Done Street.

The other, a You Pay, You Park, You Ride station
for Greyhounds,
clowns, and other fur-coat dog-pound preacher people.

One zoo is a slow walk-through zoo, a no go cart ride with
a monkey window upside down view. The other
lets destination decide

the color of a turn double turn life
style

mostly without food or fame or a frame
around this picture

of after midnight children in this Atlanta bus station.
Children too cool
to be cold
in a summer wool coat because
it matters not to most of us that

> Che Guevara was a poet, he loved Neruda.
> Che Guevara was a pickpocket, he picked his own pocket.
> Che Guevara was a doctor, he graduated medical school
> in 1953, but
> the Bolivian Army summarily executed him in the front
> yard of a school yard
> at 1:10 p.m. October 9, 1967
> Che Guevara, a poet, shot down as easy
> as a backdoor stepdog.

Pick up the book. Turn to any page. Look at me.
I am intrigued
by the rhetoric of waiting, intrigued by the demographic of
watching bus night bus station people

slow down and slow dance to the low slow music of not
quite yet knowing, going
nowhere. I, too, am here dancing my hatdance blue,
wearing my hatdance coat with holes in the sleeves of
my life,
broke

as the science of my own not knowing. This is
the high cost of cheap cool. The chemistry of life

down here at this bus station place,

fast pace, a dog race
fast forward
in the no change back, no rewind

no exchange, no refund freeway lane of not.
        Thirteen niggers sitting on the back porch
        drinking *Kool Aid.*

Salt makes almost anything
taste better. Harsh

cannot describe this suitcase life illusion without
the help of 17 other overused adjectives. Children

after midnight dragging blankets too used up
and too used out to cover the rock and the roll
of a torn soul

music. Smell the frigid night fighting air.
There is a desert war going on somewhere
in the hard wooden seats of this station.
Children
exhaling the fumes of dog smoke because
it matters not to most that
        Che Guevara born in Argentina.
        Che Guevara, a Cuban guerilla.
        Che Guevara, a Marxist Revolutionary.
        Che Guevara, a Motorcycle Diary
        Che Guevara executed summarily.
        Che Guevara, nothing now but a
        t-shirt on a street in Barcelona,

Spain.

Within the context of being out of my own context,
I speed up and talk fast in distorted feedback. Things rock
in then things rock out
and into this winter
bus station
in Atlanta
at 3 a.m. People lined up on a wall, photographs.

Grapes of bus station wrath, Dust Bowl valley.
Walker Evans walking in black and white.
A 1933 Metropolitan Museum, but
this ain't no art museum. This is life, and
I'm younger than Neil Young.

Bus station
winter cold
winter dry
winter dead, but

that's not exactly what I said. What I said was

this is the price we all pay
for the line and the lure
that reels us all in until

we are all dizzy. There's whiskey on the breath of this bus
station tonight. No!
I do not want my shoes shined at 3 a.m. in the morning.

They say it's illegal to wear a Che Guevara t-shirt
in Little Havana, Miami, Florida.

I wear mine in this bus station.

Half of the people know exactly who he is.
Half of the people do not exactly give a damn.
Half of the people do not know who he is
and the other half don't know who they are.

There you have it. Four halves equal two hotdogs
all the way save the onions.

I can feel the motion of the crowd but
the air over the rush is calm. The sweet rush of

a hurricane without a name hovering
like a chopped up helicopter
hovering

over the center of itself,
a hurricane
hurrying
up the coast of
some girl's not so pretty prom night dress.

> Thirteen niggers sitting on the back porch
> drinking *Kool Aid*

I will not confess to the crimes I've committed. No,
I do not want my shoes shined.
I'm wearing Birkenstocks for the sake of Peter Tosh
and Bob Marley. No Woman, No Cry.
Try Jah love. I did.

Let me be honest with you while I lie to you. A girl

just like you broke my soul

music, Sam Cooke, "Another Saturday Night and I Ain't ..."
and
Otis Redding, justa Sitting on the dock of San Francisco Bay
watching the tide roll away.

Bus station Bud
conceited in the pocket of his plaid sport coat
dancing a
Kentucky rainy night juke box dance,
a real hatdancing hitchhiking fool like me
without a job or shoes,

trying to figure out the blue in the blues
in the abstract eyes
of an abstract Confederate soldier still marching, 1865,
abstract from Chattanooga to Atlanta.

William Tecumseh Sherman

named after a box of matches. Close cover before striking.
Warning.

Somebody burned down a whole lotta black churches
in Alabama last week.

Bus station church sermon, fire and brimstone,
completely optional. 1865, the end of ...

if you choose not to count the empty space between
the lines and the lines of
after midnight children and grape juice diluted people.

Bus station people just passing through.

An unharvested snake in a sharkskin suit.
Three people from *People Magazine,* one from
National Geographic nursing milk not from a bottle.

Midnight cowgirls roping steer in a bottle of
Texas tall beer. And over here next to nothing,

midnight cowboys ride fences as far away as Fargo,
North Dakota. Badlands
is a national park in this bus station
tonight.

College kids too white and too rich to know which
concept to lean on first, so tonight they sleep silent as
a backpack next to a sleeping bag left at Woodstock.
Hole in the soul of another Birkenstock tennis shoe.

Bus station people just passing through.

A man in a tight black suit.

Mexicans not from Mexico, but I know
the color of hunger. I know the color of not being able
to find work. I know the color of Christian bookstores
and border patrols and
police dogs

trained only to sniff out the refried smell of refried beans.
I know exactly how

the West was won. Flashback Jesse James

and Brother Frank robbing the Great Train Robbery.

> Thirteen niggers sitting on the back porch
> drinking *Kool Aid.*

Flashback Billy not a Kid anymore, the fastest gun
in this bus station room whipping his thing around
like a gun.

All things blazing black dark
in spite of all these multi-colored leaving Thisville lights
lighting up this theater of operation as far away

as the desert soldiers seated at parade rest in seats
numbered uniformly.

US Army.com
Be All You Can Be

measured
by the number of desert people you signed up
to shoot
and kill.

Two black boot strings tucked in
to the soul of
one black boot. Sandman and Sandy Ann
eat an after-midnight snack. Desert fried
chicken comes night calling
in a desert brown box

full of buses going in and going out of
Islamic focus. Cowboys,

Indians, and soldierboys and girls next door.
And they, always they

keep telling us this is how the West was won. But I know

somewhere between dream and illusion,
somewhere between
switch on and switch off, a thin true light shines

upon the 1954 American war without words.
Brown never did
defeat the Board of Undertakers disguised
as Lawmakers.

The Greyhound bus driver does not care what
bus the little black bus children ride and

the paper flying flyer said
BE BLESSED IN JESUS'S NAME.
Call for directions.
Cell phone. Call which Jesus?

The one that sat in the back of the bus with Miss Rosa Parks
for thirty years or the one that whispered to her one afternoon,

"Don't ya move, Miss Rosa," or

the one with the blonde hair on the *Watch Tower* cover of …
or the one down on Main Street tonight drunk
as this dizzy bus station room full of gray god smoke
where

Greta Garbo acts as if she doesn't know

the sweet silent silence
in the naked sweet blonde beauty of Marilyn Monroe.

Where
the Harmonica Ladies are so afraid they are afraid
to be
afraid.
Pick up the book Jesusville, white ladies, daughters of
a confederacy of dunces and Jefferson Davis glances.

Pick up the book.
Turn to any page. In the name of somebody,
look at all those

bus station people just passing through.

Black families dressed like a TV timeout commercial,
paradox in a box of refried overfried chicken livers.

White families trying to figure out why they are in
that same paradox boat box of

rebel flags on top of a white trash trailer
trash Mobile, Alabama
home located smack in the middle of Tornado Alley,
in the middle of this African American
with no dream of becoming because …

> Thirteen niggers sitting on the back porch
> drinking *Kool Aid*.

Native Americans, an American Indian,
no Geronimo drunk as the dirt

from Custer's Last Stand standing outside of
the bus way
station door station

smoking an American Eagle cigarette peace
pipe treaty.
Another TV timeout commercial break
that breaks every
promise ever prayed in the U.S. Constitution.

Bus station people just passing through.

Rap city boys, cool, pants praying to touch the ground,
wearing
a belt with no need to be
or believe in anything
but

black girls, big butts, nice girls, big butts, church girls,
big butts
and hoochie mamas with big butts
gotta dance with somebody. And then there's

Twisted Sister
and her twisted brother wrapped around each other
because their twisted mother twisted her way

away
from their triple twisted fucked up father because
his father and his mother, too, were as twisted

as twisting up some blue Kentucky wild grass across
the street from the bus station

cabs without stands wait for hard luck strangers
and preachers needing a ride because
it matters not to most that

> Che Guevara was a poet and panhandler.
> Che Guevara, pocketknife in a pocketbook.
> A volume of Neruda's poetry found
> in his dead knapsack pocket.
> Che Guevara shot down like a backdoor step dog.

The after midnight children now asleep in the arms of
no breakfast in this America. Super Tramp
was wrong.

Lizzie
and the Rainmaker outside making love
out of nothing but
cigarette butts and bus station smoke.
A man in a tight black suit.

The moon never said anything mean to anyone.

But this ain't no story 'bout no Johnny Rotten.
This is a story about two race track dogs and a night at
the Atlanta bus station after midnight zoo.

Whiskey on the ticket taker's breath makes the whole
world slightly off-angled dizzy.

Undercover cop asleep on top of the sheet. Crime
in the street comes inside. Hey Mister.

You talking to me? Yeah you, Hey Mister

got some reds, best pill in my pocket tonight.
What about some pinks or a yellow tab of
orange sunshine. Make ya feel like the Golden Gate
Bridge fogged in like Alcatraz Island.

Hey Mister.
Do ya need some medical marijuana?
I'm a doctor, Mister.

Hey Mister.
Do you need the time?
I got some pretty witches and watches watching
the decision clock. Tick Mister tock.

Hey Mister.
wannna roll with this Rolex for a hundred and a half?
Thirty-five dollars just for you, Mister.
Hey Mister.
Do you drink Coca cola or Pepsi?
Got some Diet Coke and a spoon, Mister
if you are in—ter—est—ed, Mister.

Capitalism in an American bus station
is the title for this song.
Hey Mister.
For a good time follow me
is a pretty voice of what may or
may not be a woman.

Hey Mister.
wanna spend some time?
No

I do not want my shoes shined.
I need a lift, a forklift, and a ski lift.
I need a drink.

"Hey hey, my my. Rock 'n Roll will never die."
Neil Young on the radio,
and I'm choking down noise from a vending machine,
peanut butter crackers.

Where is that walking liquor store
airport airline airplane size bottle
walking whiskey boy?

I need a drink.
I need to fly like an astronaut. I need to buy
some freeway bus route tickets so
I can see the cross section
of this 1956-2006 night at this drive-in movie zoo.

Thirteen niggers sitting on the back porch
drinking *Kool Aid.*
Bus station people just passing through.

A Christian Science Christian girl with a wet hair smile
trying to convince me that the moon revolves
around her and I believe her
according to the Book of Just Looking
at her legs.

Vintage clothes define and classify
the early swing of early morning,
a dreadlocked blonde 17-year-old bomb

not wearing the hint of any kind of shell
as far as this Elvis boy can tell by the smell of

voodoo cooking in the bus station kitchen smoking,
Haitian red beans
and nice
zombie easy black tragic music. A pretty woman
with a bus ticket to Holy Wood, Alabama in her hand.

Roy Orbison standing in the restroom doorway
wearing sunglasses black as black is black looking
at the same pretty woman because
it matters not to most that

> Che Guevara was a poet, the spirit of self sacrifice.
> Che Guevara was a prophet and a philosopher,
> a phenomenon and a phantom,
> a paradox and a cult hero.
> Che Guevara now reduced
> to a red star on a black beret
> on the t-shirt I'm wearing tonight.

They say it's illegal to wear a Che Guevara t-shirt in Miami.
Winter nights are not kind to cold water weather people
and/or the science of being simply warm. The dark side

of the harvest moon is lost in the relationship between
Neil Young and a Nine Inch Nail, lost
in the dropback backdrop smoke of too many smoke break

cigarettes. Pink Floyd, the dark side, The Who.
Pete Townsend, who are you smashing
that guitar like

the Smashing Pumpkins?

Who are you? The question we all asked ourselves before
walking away from the bus station restroom
morning mirror madness.

Get on any bus. Let destination decide the color of the ride.

Those drifter days are here again and again
I am running against a night too bright
with uneasy uneven destination lights.

History lesson 101 on a 4-way street. May 4th
one nine seven zero
4 Dead in Ohio. Neil Young on the radio in Nashville.

Marlon Brando and James Dean up on the movie screen.
Everyone in this place is leaving except the ticket taker's
pocketbook. Let

the Harley boys
ride on outta here,

ride right through the middle of this bus station
and on out into
the night on a highway west of wherever

where that girl is wearing those god-awful red
alligator boots,
legs white as a 1963 Chevy Impala.

Hey Mister, look at the way this world spins tonight.

Bus station people just passing through.

Baseball caps and homegrown hometown college teams.
March marching mad in the faces of a few.

A Rose Bowl t-shirt
noon day parade floating over the grave
of James Marshall Hendrix. LSD Lucy in the Sky t-shirt
with too many Diamonds
in disguise.

> Thirteen niggers sitting on the back porch
> drinking *Kool Aid.*

Bus station people just passing through.

NBA NFL oversized jerseys, rap cap music
dance, can't sit still in the required stillness
of a bus station seat next to another
bus station seat. It would be nice to get something
to eat.

A black man in a tight black suit.

Bus station people just passing through.

Some read newspapers, some read the same novel
you would be reading if you were in this bus station
state of mind.
Some read each other as if to say …

my state of homelessness is better than your
state of homelessness. As if to say …

an expensive big screen TV came in my cardboard
box bus station home without a ticket.

Arrivals and departures echo, breaking the stillness of
unstill after-midnight air.

Snakes do not hibernate in a winter bus station zoo.
A shark in snakeskin suit selling wolf tickets to wolves
in faux fur coats.

This world is square tonight.

"Monday, Monday" on the after-midnight stereo.

People with torn apart lives stumbling through
fields stranger than Lady Day Billie Holiday fruit.
The Clock
ticks nothing but hard empty numbers.

Bus station people, hard people dancing
to the uneven beats of a hard uneven life.
A girl just like you broke my soul.

Bus station people laughing and laughing and laughing
because
it matters not to most that

> Che Guevara was poet, a philosopher, a paradox,
> and a poet. But
> then a postscript poet left dead in the street
> like a step street dog.

Holly, you, go lightly girl, Tiffany's is closed

for the rest of this life.
Drag on drag queens of the morning dragging in what
somebody dragged out.

The needle and the damage done. Neil Young
in Nashville
sued by the record label for not sounding like
Neil Young.
But this ain't no story 'bout no Johnny Rotten.
This is revolution
untelevised

a bus, an army station, an army base in the face
of a killing grin,
a soldier boy, maybe 17, dressed in Marine dress blue. Green

Peace is a lie.
Too many green faces carved into a black reflecting pool
wall in Washington, reflecting dead dog track tickets
and dead Kennedys.

The centrifugal coolness of my sweet words turn
bitter and bite,
and I litter my conversation with expressions from the wrong
Bob Dylan song.
Tangled up in blue
like
Sick Dick
and the Volkswagens, an English group
nobody believes in anymore
than I believe in the ordered swirl of buses
and boxes.

Close the door, Neil,
turn out the lights.
Jim Morrison is dead.

SIX

FREEWAY EXITS AND A ONE TREE PARKING LOT

ESSAY

NO EASY SILENCE

(Rain Sleep Truck, Walmart Parking Lot)

Since I was a little boy, people have told me that something was wrong with me. Odd little dark skinned-boy, I guess I was just a bit, considering the odds stacked up against the other odds of my young, sometimes life. Something wrong with me? I can't say I've ever known the true definition of that uneasy definition of myself. Maybe it was my solid childhood attention to the Negro gospel, trembling voice of Elvis, shaking the whole world like a 1961 stubborn quake. Maybe it was not the shaking at all. Anyway, tonight finds me fogged in with the beautiful arrogance of the Dixie Chicks, taking the long, wrong way home. I'm "A Thousand Miles from Nowhere," contemplating time and place constructed to the specific angles of a four letter word with one vowel. The single voice of Natalie, Martie, and Emily is dancing a cut in an American made rug, and the blood is spilling as far away as Texas. Everything and all things tonight are braced up against the advantage of hard falling rain, and I'm trying to fall asleep without closing my eyes. The rain, the road, the radio do not know the mathematics of crying or the language of clouds. Perhaps because I do, a logical argument can be made to fall between the lines of an illogical perspective on this illogical night, folded back flat in hard times and London fog.

On top of my sleeping bag, still as a still pan of still water, I'm alternating between looking up at the ceiling and looking out from the rear window view of my Infiniti QX4. In the not-so-distant future, a storefront sign announces, "Walmart," but her always-open-ended voice is just as distorted as my view is drained by the pour of rain from a plastic blue bucket. It's the third Tuesday in the month of June, and the sky is more than falling out of sorts with this city tonight. I've been parked here in this parking lot just long enough to distantly discern, "This is not a walking man's town." Listening to the trajectory of my life defined by the design of freeway noise, Sheryl Crow is playing a concert in an open field on my little transistor radio. I brought it along not for the ride, but because as a kid we lived in a tin roof radio shack with a single window view. Looking out was forever draped by kind, but dirty, white curtains that never quite let in enough sun or enough light.

That transistor radio was the only thing Grandmama ever really owned. She raised me on that radio. I can see her now, listening to WMFD on the dial of rainy nights in that tin roof shack where she and I lived along the edge of Highway 17, the last highway on the east coast of my growing up years. Hampstead, North Carolina was smaller than any dot on any map. Our shack was just a ways back, maybe 20 yards, from the George Washington Memorial Live Oak Tree. According to words carved and placed in granite by the Daughters of the American Revolution, Washington and his men stopped to rest at my rest stop on a night in 1776. Gypsies, goat cart tramps, and other George and Martha Washingtons all stopped at my rest stop to rest and wrestle the poverty of being too poor to go on. Eventually, like us, they all got back into their cars and onto their carts and moved on, just as poor as before.

For five winters, Grandmama and I lived there in the shade of that road side stop, happy as we were permitted to be on the front porch of a no porch house until the year of that extra summer came and the ice thawed.

Tonight, stretched out in back of a breaking breeze, it is with the unease of not forgetting that I remember the first of winters when sleep wrapped me warm, and my dreams were not frigid and bitten by frost. It was the winter of my first grade. I had to leave Grandmama and our shack when I started school. She stayed, and I moved to the city, as far away from George Washington as I had ever been. Living in Jervay Housing Projects, twisting and turning beneath sheets of radiator heat, my life, for a while, walked backwards down unsweet streets. I missed the sweet smell of sweet corn growing, but I adjusted the dials. Adjustment without improvement comes with a price, sometimes not so obvious from what the price tags say. The original markdown price was still way too expensive for all the angry, hungry, happy, laughing people living in bricks of red contradiction. City life had no frame to its unsacred disguise. It was exactly what it was, the undefined definition of radio sociology in the streets of African America. Number runners running in rhythm, pimps pimping, short sleeve shirt thieves selling blue jeans, welfare checks checking out and cashing in on dead "you figger" people, and the constipation of too much government issued cheese and peanut butter, all mainlined into the heroin hungry veins of too many of the people I knew.

And then there was the harsh happiness of us, nappy headed kids running wild, running to find the meaning of life outside of meaning intended, lost at the onset, lost to the unsavory order of color coordination and arrangement. I did not know then, at seven years old, why I was so concerned with the spinning colors of spinning things. In the wake of a hurricane marriage, my mother left us for the bright lights of another hard luck town. My father stayed, broken as his own broken down gray Chevrolet. That car never did figure out how to start two days in the same week. The calm eyes of Grandmama became the eyes of high windy rain. She blew us out of town, you might say. She took us, five brothers, to live on what once was a farm, in what once was a house at the dark shadowed end of a small fishing community. Hampstead, North Carolina in 1961 was as all white as an all white Presbyterian church. There we lived at the edge of a ticking time clock until the ice thawed again.

So on this night of steady hard falling rain, lying flat in the back of my SUV in the parking lot of an all-night open Walmart located somewhere between Raleigh and Durham, North Carolina, I find myself remembering the obvious, "Boy, something is wrong with you," echoing in through fogged-in windows. But the thing is, I have a bottle of Kentucky Jack, and it's raining everything tonight but dogs and definitive definitions. Walmart midnight parking lot, half full or half empty, depending on the psychological state of the view finder's choice. The freeway is as close as the toss of two long touchdown passes down field. The rainy night air is cool, and the radio is full of itself. "Rikki don't lose that number," a decade of Steel, low blasting my life along on what seems an uncharted path to nowhere. The road and the radio on a night of no dance music watch as the dog days of raining thought sit quietly between my comfort and my pain. The meaning of life reduced to puddles in a parking lot road. Dead silence refuses to say a word, and the dashboard lights are asleep at the wheel. Beads of water reflect and refract parking lot pole night lights, casting a trillion tiny beams, rolling down windows of this life like a trillion tiny gods. The drums of Indians dance upon the roof, steady as wild horses galloping across an open desert floor. The Cherokee used to be here at the edge of these foothills. They are gone now. Just names now: Navaho Trail, Shawnee Drive, Cherokee Avenue. Street names and road signs now, Native America reduced to the price of a museum ticket. Looking out from my fogged-in window view, I see no Tecumseh star and no Crazy Horse moon.

In spite of the works of fire, flash dancing all along the aisle and alleyways of this freeway world, there is no celebration here. Tonight, in my own limited space, alone, I find myself too many miles away from Chattanooga, Tennessee, where I now live and teach at the University. I was making good travel time, speeding along interstates of rain, buzzing on a fresh cup of Zip Store coffee, when I heard what I thought I heard. Exit 101, the intersection of poetry and politics, called out clear. Yet, I barely heard the subtle silent spaces between the letters of my first name whisper, "Stop here." So I stopped, and here I am, listening to the idea of being happy to be alone and afraid, confused by storm clouds. Perhaps my frequency should be as honest as the radio voice frequency of Marvin Gaye, moaning, "What's going on" then with the refrain of hard falling rain, "War is not the answer." I have seven cousins, too removed to name, in Iraq and Afghanistan. What frequency, I wonder, are they listening to tonight in their desert sand of little-to-no measurable rain?

This roof of steady hard rain steals my mind and pushes it back. I remember nights of listening to summer showers falling with the ease of easing every pain in my small world. As they say, "Life was so simple" when summers were baseball games behind the church, and every black preacher was a light-skinned, handsome man who drove a Cadillac into town on Sunday morning and out of town on Sunday afternoon, and the congregation paid for that Cadillac without question because they believed Jesus was that man in that picture, behind the pulpit, never hung straight. Lies cannot be hung straight, anyway. It was a time when Sunday would not be Sunday without fried chicken after church, and no funeral would be the end of a life without fried fish after the dead were laid to rest. Hampstead and the surrounding Negro communities were evenly placed places, unwritten in rules that separated drinking water, separated cemeteries, separated schools and churches for psychological comfort and the easy understanding of borders.

But I was a borderless child. I know now as I knew then, borders were invented by makers of maps in the aftermath of war and words. The generals draw a line, and call it the border between two places that used to be one place. War is man-made, and the friction of war designs the fiction of everyday novels. Therefore, I am quite aware that the color of my ordinary black shirt walking toward my ordinary black car in any ordinary mall parking lot in America is a walk in sync with the click of an ordinary white car lock. Click! Every time I hear it, I hear the music of drinking a glass of ordinary water, break.

And on this no Van Gogh night, upon burning words left smoldering in the middle of the road somewhere between Raleigh and Durham, North Carolina, I'm listening to music, some of which, I've been told not to love. It's raining so hard, I climb up front to turn the windshield wipers on to make sure I'm not floating away in this crazy or is it a holy state of contemplation. According to the United States Department of Vital Statistics, a black man is not supposed to listen to and love country music, not supposed to cross the boundaries that separate music from music. I recall once having a yard sale in my front yard. Along with junk, I was selling some of my CDs. An older black man was thumbing through the collection, quite puzzled, when he asked, "Are you sure these are your CDs?" Yes, I thought, and they have always been mine. All the way back to Patsy Cline 1959, they have always been mine.

Just as there is separation outside of, there is separation within a given radio dial. A few days ago, I purchased *Taking the Long Way Home* by the Dixie Chicks. Tonight I find myself taking the wrong way home. It's foggy, it's raining, and I'm gazing into the beautiful dark shadowed eyes of Natalie Maines, the Chicks are on the cover of this week's *Time* magazine. It's the story of three Texas school girls with a history of selling more records than any Country and Western group ever. It's the story of three Texas women who happen to speak from the very heart of a ticking clock one night on a stage in London on the eve of the Gulf War. It's the story of what happens to any woman in America with the courage to place her ear to the corn silk soul of Marvin Gaye, *What's going on.*

According to *Star Watch,* Week of June 4-14, 2006, one of the more innocuous explanations given as to why country radio has not been playing the Dixie Chicks' new single, "Not Ready to Make Nice" is because the defiant song doesn't fit in with everything else that's playing on the dial. More to the voice of my own point, I remember that fateful night in March 2003, on the eve of the Iraq invasion, when the voice of Natalie jumped out from the dark and told that London audience that she was ashamed that George W. Bush, the President of the United States, hailed from Texas. Natalie's words spotlighted a chasm between the Chicks and the country music industry, a chasm between those of us who know war is not the answer and those of us still fighting in Vietnam, a chasm between those of us who know John Lennon had a beautiful voice, and those of us who stood to deport him because his wire-frame glasses were round.

There is no easy way out on this night of torrential rain. Some things are too sad to remember, but we remember them anyway. I want to tell you two stories. Before I tell you the first, I'll tell you the second. Last Thursday night I handed the ticket taker my ticket and walked into a Dwight Yoakam concert. The moment I walked in, I was on center stage, beyond the center of attention. The only other black face in that place was the seemingly content profile of a man scooping cigarette butts from a cigarette butt can next to the "Maybe you shouldn't come in here" front entrance door. For the first time in my life, I thought, maybe there is something wrong with me. The borderless boy had stumbled across a hard white line without realizing the neon on that no neon night. Then I remembered eating hotdogs without fries in the kitchen of a restaurant when I was a kid. NO COLORED NEGROES ALLOWED in the dining area; it might upset the sensitive few. Being a poet radio boy, always wearing a shirt without a border or a collar, I had forgotten too many of the things I had not remembered to learn, but that night …

Now let me get this straight. I know how to add and subtract decimals. I am a faction, part African, part English, and part Cherokee. Just like almost every African American in America, I am trying to dance to my own three-part harmony. I grew up in a white town, listening to Elvis and Ricky Nelson on the radio. I played many summers of baseball in the sideyard and backyard of a white Presbyterian church. While my grandmama ironed Mrs. Cora Mae's white sheets, I played tag football with a white neighborhood full of white boys. I was always the quarterback, win or lose, I called every play. The caliber of color was never a measurement of intelligence in my mind. My childhood was happy because, in spite of all things, I never paid attention to the way drinking water was separated. Sure I went to an all black school in the early years. Sure the congregation at my church was all black. Sure I was in 8th grade before I had my first white teacher. I must have had some idea about something concrete and carved in black and white, but that night …

So I passed through the concert crowd, bordered in too tight to untangle, when I remembered Al Pacino's lines from my favorite movie, *Scent of A Woman,* " When you get tangled up, tango on." So I tangoed on up to my balcony, tangled up, front row seat, only to find that A-114 was right beside A-113 and A-113 was big, red, bald, and white and not smiling at this camera boy, slow falling in a drift upon a seat too small for the unevenness of the evening. To add to the drama of that moment, I must tell you that row letter A was unoccupied from A-15 to the end of the aisle, about eight empty seats. Seats to my right were crammed in too tight to breathe, and according to a disturbing-the-peace police report not reported, I was convicted of disturbing the peace of mind of the sensitive many.

Maybe something is wrong with me, but *amazing* is my amazing word. Years have taught me how to get people who do not want to talk to me to talk to me. It's simple. All you have to do is start asking a bunch of questions. And sooner, not later, Cowboy Roy was telling me about his many Garth Brooks concerts. Now Cowboy Roy never did ask me any questions. Cowboy Roy never learned that I served five years in the U. S. Air Force, three years in the Army National Guard, and seven months in the Naval Reserve. But somehow, he knew I burned every uniform that was ever issued to me. Intermission was intense, a different level, when the lights were up, and the spotlight spotted me as easy as eavesdropping. A woman some rows behind me said, "You know I felt like I was voting all over again when I bought that new record by the Dixie Chicks." Listening without looking, I thought about John Kerry, I thought about George W. Bush, and I thought about the space between winning and losing. From that woman's voice, I concluded that "A Thousand Miles from Nowhere" was somewhere, right there that night in that Tivoli Theatre America. And I was and am in the middle of a soldout show, tangled up in sheets of solid sounding rain, convicted for being me.

In order to tell you the first story, I have to take you back to when I truly was on the road, when I honestly warmed my soup cans with a cigarette lighter, when Jack Kerouac was my Buddha, and my backpack was my god. That summer, I crossed America three times. I hitch hiked, rode buses, rode AmTrack, flew in planes over my own cuckoo's nest, and I walked in many cities from one end to the other end. While on the road, I wrote a novel, *Looking for Jack Kerouac.* The Chicago chapter, "After Allyson" won the 1995 International Jack Kerouac Literary Prize. In the fall, I was invited to Kerouac's hometown, Lowell, Massachusetts, to receive the prize and to read the award winning chapter. Ole beaten up beatnik Herbert Huncke and "the" Patty Smith were there that weekend, but the night of my reading was my Andrew Warhola fifteen minutes. In theory, that is. That night, I read "After Allyson," the story of a black boy and a white girl who fall in love with each other's voice, and spend one night together walking the streets of Chicago, talking, falling deeper and deeper. They finally fall asleep in a vacant corner of the bus station. When he wakes, Allyson is gone. Nothing left but the smear of red lips on his forehead. After the applause, I accepted the narrow prize check and stepped back into the dark.

A faint blue light appeared when I noticed that everyone except me and a few smokers and outsiders had gone to a local bar for drinks. The awarding committee left, and we stayed, uninvited, until the light grew brighter. As fate would have it, we ended up in the same bar. Professor Who Knows nearly fell from his seat when he saw me standing there, black as Jack Kerouac's jazz Buddha. In less than the time it takes to move, they moved their party upstairs. After most had left, one drunk student stumbled up into my face, so close I smelled his whiskey from days ago. With a narrow-eyed disposition, he point-blank-pistol-shot asked, "What gives you the right to write about Jack Kerouac?"

There was no easy silence then, and there is no easy silence now. My mind is fully awake and walking a Johnny Cash line all along the watchtowers of that and many evenings, tangled up in a Dylan dark blue haze of smoldering words. Bob Seger and the Silver Bullet Band now singing on my little transitor radio, asking me, of all people, if I want to go to "Fire Lake." Believing all things are beautiful has always been my fatal mistake. I think I'll take the voice of my own unflinching reason to the concrete Chicago shores and dance, just one moment, in the heat of "Fire Lake."

I could be wrong, but I believe that I am not. If you are going to shoot Natalie, Martie, and Emily, then pickup your shotgun, Mr. Mister and shoot me. Shoot me for being born in America with a shadow over my face. Shoot me for being blind to the geography of maps and borders. Shoot me for learning the lyrics of my love song. Shoot me for figuring on my fingers the mathematics of a world without war. Shoot me for ignoring the slanted science of one-way stop signs and dead end streets. Shoot me for not paying attention to the biology of musicology and color-coded design. Shoot me and lay me to rest in the best Best Western movie John Wayne and John Ford ever made, then bury my wounded heart at Wounded Knee right between Red Cloud and Crazy Horse. No flowers please. Just let me RIP.

This night has become way too sad for sleep. I remember my grandmama used to say, "Lord what is this world coming to?" I don't know, Grandmama. All I know is that all those freeway bumper stickers you see these days that say "God Bless America" have no intentions of meaning "God Bless All America." The cruel designs of cartography mark our days from the very beginning. Some of us are in, and some of us are not. It's like the Russian Poet Yevtushenko said when I told him the story of my Lowell, Massachusetts defeat, "At first we form the borders and then they, the borders, form us." I see now Grandmama, with uneasy eyes, that perhaps it has always been my simple, honest understanding of the principles of mapmaking that constitutes what's wrong with me.

The rain has now slowed to an uneven drizzle in the unsacred Walmart woods of Uncle Sam Walton, but the dark clouds of crows are not gone. They are hovering over the reasons men so easily go to war and so easily are killed. I can barely hear the weak batteries pushing John Lennon to sing just a bit louder, "Give peace a chance." No need to turn off the radio. The music is dying on its own. "And we were singing *bye bye, Miss American Pie, drove my Chevy to the levee, but the levee was dry.*"

Slowly, the morning world is starting to turn. Streets are starting to crowd. I need a cup of coffee. In the distance, I see three choices and three tall signs. The peeking-out-of-an-apple red sun promises a beautiful blue North Carolina day. In an hour or so, Grandmama, I'll be on my way, for the rest of my life, wrong or right, taking my own way home. And the roads I know not so well after all will dance, until all at once and as one, the white lines that separate coming from going will blur in the rearview like an orchestra, C minor, blue and flat as roads through mountains refuse to be.

SEVEN

HIGH-YELLOW NIGHT NIGGER ROADS

MONKEY JUNCTION, 1969

Scoping John Thomas Scopes and the Nature of His Trial

Where the name came from?
I don't know. Perhaps this place
was properly improperly
named in sacred honor of the sacred
monkey scope colored nature
of the promise and the people
that spooned out and forked up

the contours of that or this
high-yellow
night nigger
smooth dark road.

William Jennings
Bryan and Clarence Darrow and Mr.
Charles must have lived
quite handsomely there

in a convertible dead-road-ahead car
years before I was
born, 12 miles to the north. If you
take the road from
Wilmington toward Carolina Beach,
a flashing yellow
light will slow your yellow car
down, and a white shaking
sign with black shaking letters
will tell you where you are.

Monkey Junction, at the intersection of.
Even if you look closely, still, you will not be,

without black sunglasses, able to clearly see
the sign:
NO NIGGERS ALLOWED AFTER SUNSET
written sideways on a billboard, hanging
from the sky.

When I was a kid I saw the sky and I knew
it was covered
by a very big black woman. A woman,
the blue berry picking people called
Miss Monkey.
Miss Monkey had four children.
One I liked, one I kinda liked
and two who did not like
the way I looked between the pages
of my science book. The theory
of my evolution evolved
one summer hot day
in the back seats of a blueberry bus.

There was a fight, and there I was
wearing boxer shorts in the center
of a boxed-in-solid three ring circus
sized boxing ring.

Four against one, me.
Three brothers and one sister.
Big Miss Monkey's cornfield children
cornered me
in. My back to the very back
of a coward circus
blue bus. Dull kitchen, dull knife
resting on my throat. Sharp

switchblade cut
across my left arm.
That scar, now a birthmark,
all the proof needed
for the scope
of the Scope's Monkey trial.

The theory of evolution
by natural selection selected
the shirt I was wearing that day of
all the days
I wore the ragged same
blueberry picking,
cotton picking shirt
to the blueberry fields of my youth.

Jesus must have picked me to be
the one to figure the mathematics of
what could not be. So
I put together two idiots plus two
idiots plus three
back of the bus seats
plus four o'clock in the afternoon
and came up fighting, writing
on the wrong side
of my school boy notebook sheet of
white paper.

Came up with the wrong wide
measured angle to technically knockout
the electricity
in the eyes of nothing to be
behold. My right upper cut

and my left cross
hook were too quick
to explain in logical fashion how
the shirt I was wearing could ever fit
me as well as it fit into the relationship
between William Jennings
Bryan and Clarence Darrow
and the blinking yellow light,
and Mr. Charles Darwin
struck at the fork.
John Thomas Scopes
was a high school teacher, trying to teach
a science class. Miss Monkey
and her children were plowed under
people left behind like October corn poles.
"Inherit the Wind" was a 1955 play,
staged without a prayer or a plot.

MRS. DAVIS

The Question of Race War: To Be or Not to Be

Miss Davis wasn't Negro black
like Black Moses or Miles Dewey Davis,
but she had a trumpet
in her voice, hard, sweet, and cold
as the way Miles played a slow
"It Never Entered My Mind."

Horn rimmed librarian glasses
unevenly clinging onto the very tip
of her angled English rose
nose. She farm plowed and pushed
a field full
of books, hurriedly
like a library shelf, burning down
knowledge.

7:45 to 3:15, Monday through Friday
at John T. Hoggard High School
was race war riot before, during,
and between clashes
and classes of black and white
cafeteria trays and
the bad, hard ways of boys and girls
without
entrées on paper sack menus that
flatly refused to promise anything
beyond
the promise of fire
and the burnt smell of street life
smoke.

Under the flag and banner of no fear,
steadfast,
she taught Shakespeare till Shakespeare,
himself, shook
the classroom walls. Arithmetic days

rained rocks, and arithmetic nights
poured kerosene and gasoline onto the flames.
Every white owned store in our neighborhood
burned.

Police imposed curfews told us not to
come outside
when police helicopters
were dropping notebook
colored teargas onto the clothes
on clotheslines
in my backyard, but God
had a louder voice so
we listened, but not to the stars
or the sad crescent
of an uncaring sad moon, knowing
that if, in fact,
Neil Armstrong did, in fact, walk
on the moon, he was still up there
and we were still down here

with knots on our heads
from listening
to the tick-tock-tick night
Negro night stick disguised
by and in
the indistinguishable rhythm

rhyme of a trigger
happy policeman, quite happy
and much obliged
to send any one of us straight
to the gates
in a cheap grey dog bus box. Yet
from the Shakespearean
pages of Shakespeare, himself,
Mrs. Davis recited
a tragedy in first person, while
the separated city erupted red,
exploded
and burned the spelling words
right off of the pages of
the spelling book without
mispronouncing
the name,
Wilmington, North Carolina
burning
block by block after block
all the way up
and including the very steps
of city hall.

Yet through it all,
all was always cool calm
in English classroom 222.
"To be or not to be,"
was never a question.

THE CHEROKEE IN ME

Between the chapters of slavery,
seventeen birthdays have counted
the seventeen pages. I remember
the sad shape of ships and storefront
signs swinging
in the noon day of a horrible sun. Time
and heritage stands
still for the people who are darker than
dark blue. You would not believe
the sound or the smell of cotton
seed dust. Back we go, when we step back
into a history that's not history at all.
Fall feels like spring,
when trees forget to change
the color of this world. Everything, they say,
connects now to seasons of no rain. My life
is made of cityscape snow,
and I promise you absolutely nothing
but reasons that refuse to explain
the things I do not know.
In the sacred hills above my head,
a red Cherokee
rides into a red night on a red pony.
Grandmama said the people called
her father Indian nigger, and she
said, they called her, behind her back, half
Indian nigger. The bones
of my cheeks rise to meet
the war paint my father
painted everyday he scaled fish,
every night he drove fish trucks, and every
time he danced
to the call of his own name,

calling him to load more fish boxes
boxing him into believing
what he could not believe. My mother
believed him for as long as she could.
But fish-truck-patience has a way
of running out and running into
the strides of wild horses
captured
on reservations of the mind.
Red people walked all the way
to Oklahoma. Red people tracking
red Georgia clay as they marched,
and
the cotton seed dust danced
the cotton-seed-dance, and chance
to become
became the valley of my ship wrecked
heritage, tracked in snow.

EIGHT

STREET CORNER BOYS AND TWO INTERSECTIONS ON A DEAD END ONE-WAY

THE WILMINGTON TEN

(A Novel)

Prologue:
Wilmington Star News. Wilmington, North Carolina
The loud-ass, crazy, first few days of the cruel, cold,
uncaring, slow talking, month of February, 1971.
Headlines:

The Wilmington 10

Any 9 of them could've been
any 9 of us.
Any 1 of them could've been me.

The Wilmington 10

9 black boys and 1 white woman
convicted,
arrested,
convicted,
tried,
convicted again.
Arson and Conspiracy,
The Fire
bombing of
Mike's Grocery
February 6, 1971, the year of the gun.

The Wilmington 10

convicted and sentenced to a combined
282 years
in prison.

200 years for this,
80 years for that and
2 years for good measure, I suppose.

Table of Discontent.

Nine dark skinned
chapters plus one
fair faced paragraph
all on page number 1

"Who dun it" was never a question
in the voices of too plenty to name.
By all broken night streetlight accounts
it was a sad twisting newspaper account
except for those who actually did
the counting, 123456789 and 10.

The second month of the year
of our Lord, 1971
was a cruel and cold, uncaring time
to be stranded between the yellow
pages of phone book numbers
and the *Wilmington Star News*
newspaper account of the name count.

On the day in question
all traffic stopped
in a confused halt, blocked
and blindsided.
Gun shots were ringing
doorbells up and down side streets
and alley ways.

Church bells were calling out
to the nonbeliever
in the name of the same
our Lord of perpetual
1971 lies.

White citizens, locked up
in white people luxury.
Black citizens, barricaded
in red brick house poverty.
Black sniper boy, supposedly,
on the roof
of the Gregory Congregational Church.

Black church
Black neighborhood
Black Amen corner pew
with a white preacher
named Eugene.
Should've been clean enough
to wear to Sunday school but
it was not
the right time of year.

The ROWP (Rights of White People)
and KKK (no explanation needed)
on patrol downtown looking for
a reason to shoot a nigger when
they really didn't need a reason or
a good paying, killing job
or a warm clean bloody sheet
to sleep like we did between the red
bricks of government issued

red hot radiator heat.

February 6, 1971 at approximately
WHEN
Mike's Grocery store was firebombed,
Black sniper
boy, supposedly, fired from the roof
of an unfaithful church
and the bullets without names
followed some other god
down into the face
of a white fireman and he danced
a white fireman dance
around and around in white circles of
uncivil hot white light.

Implications, full of lying night snake oil
and smoke billowing out from behind
the black neck bones of damage
already done
1 times 10 equals 10
in the city of Wilmington, North Carolina.

The National Guard came 2 days later
than the alligator, still lying and telling lies
in the winter day afternoon sun
on the bloody banks
of the Cape Fear River, reliving the history of
1898 in Wilmington, North Carolina.

9 plus 1 also equals 10
convicted.
Arson and conspiracy in connection with

whatever a fool connects another fool with.

That foggy Wilmington, North Carolina morning
still a vivid memory for me and a world that refused
to see beyond the smoke of Mike's Grocery Store.

Chapter 1.
The Reverend Benjamin Chavis Jr., age 24.
Convicted
34 years with good behavior,
a man's life without.
Brother Ben, a beautiful brother,
beautiful afro.
Arrested more than 30 times before
the Oxford North Carolina United Church of Christ
sent him down to our town. I knew him well,
marched to the steps of city hall with him.
All the girls loved him.
He had green snake charming church boy eyes,
deadly as a gun, 1971.

Chapter 2.
Connie Tindall, age 21.
Convicted
31 years with good behavior,
a man's life without.
Connie Boy, a big black boy, a bully.
I didn't like him
or his brother and if he had a sister,
I didn't like her
either. He was the one who knocked me out,
cold
at the 10th yard line Turkey Bowl

tackle football game.
Thanksgiving Day 1970 saw everything
coming.
I just didn't see Connie Tindall
coming out of the backfield.

Chapter 3.
Marvin "Chili" Patrick, age 19.
Convicted.
29 years with good behavior,
a boy's life without.
We all called him Chili cause he was cold
and cool. Chili
was a real Oakland, California Black Panther.
He wore a black beret sideways
like Huey P. Newton,
had freckles like a white boy,
a real revolutionary brother.
Reminded me of George Jackson
sleeping with Angela Y. Davis.

Chapter 4.
Wayne Moore, age 18.
Convicted.
29 years with good behavior,
a boy's life without.
Everyone called him Wayne Mo,
you know like,
"mo better," but wasn't any better
than any of us
project street boys who refused to be
church boys
because church boys were too weak

for the winter nights
of 1971. The question: The Bible or a gun?

Chapter 5.
Reginald Epps, age 18.
Convicted.
28 years with good behavior,
a boy's life without.
Reggie, always standing around looking.
He got sucked in
to wearing pants too big
for the smallness of his fit,
just another bystander standing by
waiting for the revolution to start.

Chapter 6.
Jerry Jacobs, age 19.
Convicted.
29 years with good behavior,
a boy's life without.
Jerry played tennis like he was
The French Open,
aced every serve except
the last one, double
fault. Wasn't his fault, sidewalks
naturally crack.
Said he was my cousin and I believed him.

Chapter 7.
James "Bun" McCoy, age 19.
Convicted.
29 years with good behavior,
a boy's life without.

Honey Bum had a voice that thundered,
loud
as the bass guitar he played like Hendrix,
the god of all guitars. He loved a girl
named Joyce and a girl named Joyce
loved him like no love I've ever seen
in the movies or on television.

Chapter 8.
Willie Earl Vereen, age 18.
Convicted.
29 years with good behavior,
a boy's life without .
Willie Earl, he was my boy and I loved him
because he used to beat the living color out
of a set of beat up, pawn shop drums,
carried his sticks in his back pocket.
If Jesus Christ ever needed a drummer,
we all would have voted twice
for Willie Earl Vereen. Age, just 18.
He was the youngest of "The Ten."

Chapter 9.
William "Joe" Wright, age 19.
Convicted.
29 years with good behavior,
a boy's life without.
Joe Wright perfected the science of
telling a lie,
too beautiful not to believe everything
Joe Wright said
was going to be turned upside down
by the time

our world decided to stop
turning over to spill every cup
we set out to fill
in the mist of our unforgiving times.
Joe Wright
was always right.
He was the smartest of all of us.

Chapter 10.
Ann Shepard, age 35.
Convicted.
15 years with good behavior,
a woman's life without.
Ann Shepard, a fat white woman because
she was
fat and white and a woman
with a beautiful "I love colored people
personality," came down to Wilmington
from somewhere in Ohio. Other than that
I don't know what or when or where or why
our mothers didn't cry us into believing
in the good sweet whiteness. Sweet Jesus,
I just don't know.

Epilogue
The Needle and the Damage Done is a song
by Neil Young, a song singing in the red
brick breeze
in the lives of plenty, too many.
Nine boys
from among us
selected,
collected,

convicted.

We all were accessories before
the fact,
during
the fact
and after the aftermath of
that fact-
filled February night in 1971
now concealed
and sealed
in the tired writings of court room records.
President Jimmy Carter
and North Carolina Governor
Jimmy Hunt,
both, two Jimmys,
hunted and haunted without
the ability
to find,
corner and kill the nigger
hunting season legislation.
Two witnesses recanted.

A decade in jail.
Amnesty
was not international
in North Carolina in 1971,
the year of the gun.

Mike's Grocery Store was not rebuilt.
The End

NINE

TIMES
ELEVEN
EQUALS
TWENTY-THREE

BEFORE AND AFTER THE AFTERMATH: 9X11=23

The Second Assassination of John, Bobby, Abraham, and Martin

> The United States themselves are essentially
> the greatest poem. — *Walt Whitman*

Everything begins at the beginning. Therefore, the tragedy of Gotham looks
all the way back to
Y1K + 400 + 92y = $\frac{1776}{13}$ stars divided by 13 faded stripes
drapes over dead noise $\frac{\text{now}}{\text{yesterday}}$ divided by $\frac{\text{tomorrow}}{\text{if}}$
it comes

again, into that blue Gotham City morning of …
remembering how civil a civil war refuses to be.
Y1K + 800 + 65y divided by 2 = 1 nation under God

speed = $\frac{\text{distance}}{\text{time}}$ divided by $\frac{\text{time}}{\text{speed}}$ –
Times Square clock stopped
but still light travels in a straight line.

Timeline: Tyrone was still asleep. So
$\frac{\text{N}}{\text{O}}$ = no x $\frac{\text{zero}}{\text{zero}}$ at ground level zero = $\frac{\text{Man}}{\text{Hat}}$ =
Tan
black billowing
black smoke billowing into the choking history of

$\frac{\text{Pearl}}{7}$ x $\frac{\text{December}}{\text{Harbor}}$ = Y1K 941 minus $\frac{\text{FD}}{\text{R}}$ still with us, smoking a pipe

speaking, "… nothing to fear but fear itself."
POW MIA AWOL in '45,

my uncle Morris never knew why his mind never came
back home after the war.

What war, this war, another TV war, Vietnam black jungle
war not declared.

Now why then still $\frac{\text{Man}}{\text{Hat}} = \text{Tan}$
black billowing black smoke over NYC

attributable to the angry distorted distribution of

$\frac{\text{BIN}}{\text{O}}$ x 4 airline F L Ts of compressed confusion
divided by $\frac{\text{Jesus}}{\text{Allah}}$

inverted without warning to $\frac{\text{Allah}}{\text{Jesus}} \times 9 \times 11 = 23.$

Timeline: Raj had just missed his train.

The trigonometry of right triangles turned abrupt, left

and abruptly left all seats empty.

Timeline Allyson was feeding her new baby.
The captain has turned off the no smoking sign.
The sun forgot to rise above the blue trade center

Gotham City morning of …

Timeline: Sam was stuck on the LA freeway #5

Where were you?
8:46 a.m. EST X   Flight # 11   crash   divided by   WTC
dash North Tower = 92 x 1

RI   no   P   minus 1
Dead John Kennedy gunshot Dallas November
dash 22 dash   Y1K 963.

Where were you?
9:03 a.m. EST X   Flight # 175   crash   divided by
WTC dash South Tower = 65 x 1

RI   no   P   minus 2
Dead Robert Francis Kennedy gunshot L.A.   June
dash   5   dash   Y1K 968

factored into the smoke-filled graphic solution of near

Simultaneous Quadratic

explosions on NATIONAL TV. Liberty, herself, resigned
into the statue of $\frac{\text{what}}{\text{if?}}$
The captain has turned off the …

Timeline: Jane was washing breakfast dishes.
You are free to move about the cabin.
In case of an emergency, your seat cushion can
be used as a … device.

Timeline: Taniesha was dropping off the kids at day care.

9:45 a.m. EST X Flight # 77 crash divided by
8 sides of a war situation room
= 45 x 1
Dead dream Martin Luther Memphis hotel gunshot April
dash 7 dash Y1K 968
RI no P.
10:10 a.m. EST X Flight # 93 crash

divided by $\frac{\text{cornfield}}{\text{Penn State}}$ x $\frac{\text{Abraham Lincoln}}{\text{Gettysburg}}$ = 4 score

and 7y RI no P minus 4 = 19 box cutters
on SALE all for the price of …
One melodramatic movie shot
mostly on home video .

When velocity is constant, displacement varies directly
with the times and the names of
4 women minus Mary minus Jacqueline minus Ethel
minus Coretta Scott

Shot. Bullets ring out.

Timeline: Shubhada was waiting for the bank to open.

AK47 + 1 = AK48 + 2 =50 United States of confusion lowered
at one half past mast
or mass
greater than and/or equal to 19 boys.
17 + 2 or 16 + 3 or 18 + 1 all = 19 dead cigarette
boys, 19 dead night dream light boxes cut not to fit beneath

the airplane seat, perplexed
format of …

radio station TV channel
NBC
    CBS
        ABC
            FOX
                BBC

Live from New York, "This is Bryant Gumbel,
I'm down on 59th and 5th. Where are you?"

Where were you?   I was having my second cup of Starbucks.

Timeline: Freda was walking her dog
listening to headphones on the radio

93.5 FM divided by C / N square = CNN
reports 3,000 DOA

minus 1492 divided again into 1776 = 1u and 1i / 9 x 11

Light travels in a straight line.

Timeline: Amir was walking home after nightshift.

Susan was planning her third wedding.

Miss Jones was taking morning attendance.

Miss Miller was watching rerun soap operas.

Oliver was waiting for the liquor store to open.

Where were you when …

4 lines of angry air, no easy despair spills

onto FAA flight plan pages of …

You are now free to move about the cabin.

In case of an … your seat cushion can

be used as a flotation device.

ABOUT THE AUTHOR

Earl S. Braggs, UC Foundation Professor and Herman H. Battle Professor of English at the University of Tennessee at Chattanooga, is the author of *Hat Dancer Blue,* winner of the 1992 Anhinga Prize selected by Marvin Bell, *Walking Back from Woodstock, House on Fontanka, Crossing Tecumseh Street,* and *In Which Language Do I Keep Silent.* "After Allyson," a chapter from his yet to be published novel, *Looking for Jack Kerouac,* won the 1995 Jack Kerouac Literary Prize. Other awards include a Tennessee Arts Commission Individual Artist Grant and a Chattanooga Allied Arts Individual Artist Grant. Supported by Summer Fellowships from the University of Tennessee at Chattanooga, he traveled and wrote in Russia in 1998, France in 2002, and Spain in 2005. He is a native of Wilmington, North Carolina.